OPPOSITE DAY

DISCLAIMER:

OPPOSITE DAY IS A FICTIONAL SATIRE CONTAINING SEVERAL
CHARACTERS LOOSELY BASED ON PUBLIC FIGURES.

VERY FEW BIRDS WERE HARMED IN THE WRITING OF THIS BOOK.

OPPOSITE DAY

AARON BOTEE

Introduction:

THE KINGMAKERS

A gust of wind swept across the plains of Africa gaining speed as it made its way to the coast and then out to sea. This was the route of the easterly trade winds, and this particular gust of wind was on a mission to restore something that had been unceremoniously taken.

For centuries, the trade winds blew with consistency, playing an unheralded role in the world. However, with the rise of shipping, the trade winds took on the role of kingmakers. They did not rule, but quietly whispered directions behind the scenes, determining where and when rulers could expand their empires and traders could send their goods.

But humans learned how to circumvent the trade winds, first building steam engines that allowed them to travel when they wanted, and then digging canals and establishing shipping lanes that allowed them to travel where they wanted. Because humans no longer needed the trade winds' permission to travel, they no longer treated the trade winds with reverence.

Now, the gust of wind that was on its mission traveled at the perfect speed, over ocean waters that were perfectly warm, in weather conditions that were perfectly humid. As the gust traveled over the surface of the ocean, the humid air evaporated the ocean water beneath it, until suddenly the gust of wind collided with another gust of wind traveling in the opposite direction. The collision of the opposing forces shot both gusts directly up into the sky bringing the evaporated water along with them. The evaporated water rose into columns of clouds which then formed into a thunderstorm.

Over the next few days, the thunderstorm crossed the seas gaining strength from the warm water beneath it and consuming other storms along the way. As the thunderstorm traveled, it continued to gain momentum, becoming a tropical disturbance, then a tropical depression, and then a tropical storm. This is when it first received its name, Lisa, before finally achieving the status of hurricane.

Hurricanes come in all shapes and sizes. Some never grow beyond category-one, petering out with minimal impact. Some make it all the way to category-five but are deemed unworthy of landfall by the winds, who steer them out to the open ocean to burn out in near anonymity. Only the most elite hurricanes have both the will to become category-five and the support of the winds to make landfall.

These hurricanes are natural disasters, but natural disasters rarely have the impact worthy of the kingmaker title. If a natural disaster is devastating enough to be remembered, it is only remembered for the death and destruction it leaves in its immediate wake. The impacts of kingmakers, however, are felt in every sphere of society.

As Hurricane Lisa barreled down making landfall on the US Gulf Coast, its storm surge towered several feet above the now quaking concrete levees, which only a few minutes before had looked so sturdy and permanent. The one certainty about Hurricane Lisa was that it would bring immense death and destruction. But no one could have predicted that the physical damage it wrought would be a mere footnote of its legacy. Its true legacy would be the voice it gave rise to. A voice innocuous on its own, but whose meteoric rise would set off a chain of events that could bring about the final divide from which there might be no return.

3.5 YEARS AFTER OPPOSITE DAY DECLARED

The Davids (1/1)
(3.5 YEARS AFTER OPPOSITE DAY DECLARED)

David W. feverishly paced the room, avoiding the irritating sunlight which intrusively peaked through the windows. For decades he had patiently waited for the right opportunity. David W. had endlessly calculated and toiled in order to ensure that he and his partner, David G., were in a position to properly seize on the opportunity when it presented itself. Now, after all those years, that opportunity was finally here.

David W. and David G., professionally known as the Davids, were the savviest political consultants on K Street. On this particular Saturday, the Davids were in an emergency meeting with The President, trying to help him avoid an impending disaster. The election was 18 months away, and a major change needed to be made.

The President sat on a couch as David W. explained, "It's nothing she says or does. People just can't stand her. She must go."

"All polls show that anyone with a pulse can't stand her," David G. continued.

The President sat silent for a moment. He looked as though he was seriously deliberating the consequences of what the Davids were saying. Then, realizing that the Davids had stopped talking and were waiting for a response, he spoke up. "Huh? What did you say?"

In the most recent polls, even though the administration had an overall approval rating of 50 percent, Chandra Brown, the Vice President, had an approval rating of just 15 percent. Criticism of her was so vast and contradictory, it seemed to boil down to the simple fact that people just didn't like her.

Farm state swing voters thought she leaned too Liberal, Liberal voters in the South thought she was too much of a sellout for Conservative causes, and the Northeast and California base thought she stood for nothing. Most importantly, Pennsylvania housewives didn't like how she looked in pantsuits.

The Davids had been partners ever since David W. took on David G. as a junior partner. David G. was previously known as Jimmy, but changed his name to David when he joined David W. David W. insisted that Jimmy change his name to David because if he was going to be a junior partner, he had to be alike and like-minded in every way and on every topic. In that way, David W. was ahead of his time.

The Davids chose the singular pronoun to refer to himself collectively, to further solidify his like-mindedness.

Even though the Davids had been partners for at least 75 years, he did not look a day over 40. People attributed this to his religious avoidance of sunlight.

A *Politico* article nicknamed him Peanut Butter and Jelly because he were always together. As a Washington power broker, he had his share of negative publicity, but he found this article particularly offensive. He used every connection to persuade the author to retract the story. The author eventually printed a correction to the offending article and wrote how the Davids were more like Peanut Butter and Peanut Butter, or Jelly and Jelly, because he were alike and like-minded in every way. The Davids were mollified.

David W. calmly began his explanation to The President again: "I are talking about Chandra, she is dragging down the ticket. She must be replaced."

David G. then continued, "There is nothing she can say or do. A rose in her hands turns to ash."

The President vaguely remembered what the meeting was about. "Are we talking about the Black girl? Is she off the ticket? That's a shame, I liked her."

"Mr. President, you really shouldn't talk like that," David G. gently reminded the President.

"Sorry, I meant I liked they?" The President corrected in a questioning manner.

Since the declaration of Opposite Day, the only thing Americans from all perspectives agreed on was that they did not like Chandra. She somehow stood for nothing and all the wrong things. It wasn't that she was Black, and it wasn't that she was a woman, although it could have been that she was a Black woman.

The President was now fully engaged and locked in on the issue, "So, who do we replace they with?"

"Mr. President, you don't have to call her 'they.' That's not what I meant," David W. gently corrected The President.

"Huh, didn't the other David just say that?" The President felt as though he was starting from the beginning.

David G. continued the explanation, "Yes, I are alike in every way, it's why I can be in the same room as myself for prolonged periods without tearing me apart. Therefore, David and I use the singular pronoun, 'I,' to refer to I both. But Chandra does not go by 'they.'"

The President looked pensive again. Then, realizing that the Davids had stopped talking and were waiting for an answer, he responded. "Huh, what?"

Trying to avoid an endless digression, David W. attempted to refocus the meeting. "Mr. President, sorry, I believe the conversation has gotten off track. Now back to the Vice President."

The President conceded, "Yeah, you said she is out, so she is out. I don't get it. Last election you said America wanted a Black woman. Now you're saying they don't want a Black woman?"

"That's correct, Sir. They want someone who is Black and someone who is a woman, but not a Black woman. That, along with the fact that she is a nihilist who believes in all the wrong things. We really can't afford to have her on the ticket," David G. explained.

"So, who does that leave us with?" asked The President.

David G. shifted uncomfortably, "Well, Mr. President... the public feels that you are a bit … old."

"Huh?" said The President. "I am younger than you. I feel as spry as I did at 70. What do I have to do to prove it? Do I need to get up in front of the cameras and do the Lindy Hop? If The Former^4 President could play the sax, why can't I dance?"

David W., trying to avoid another digression, followed this up with, "Sir, I think we should save that for a rainy day. In the meantime, let's discuss who I have come up with as your new VP."

"Sir, do you remember the 'Hero of the Tennessee Valley'?" David G. asked.

The President thought for a moment and then shook his head no.

David W. gently reminded The President, "Sir, her name is Alice Hershe. She goes by @liceHerShe. You gave her the Presidential Medal of Freedom last year."

@liceHerShe (She/Her)

@liceHerShe looked into the camera, cheek-to-cheek with a member of her adoring public. Pursing their lips, they both said, "so blessed" right before the picture was taken.

@liceHerShe was at the tail-end of her book tour for her auto-biography, *So Blessed: How to Gain Followers and Influencer People.* Born into the Hershe vanilla fortune, she could have done nothing and lived off the 15 million followers she inherited. But that wasn't enough. She wanted a career of her own.

For years she toiled. She hated hate, liked #Blacklives, disliked #Alllives, and never spoke out against antisemitism without mentioning Islamophobia and all other forms of hate. Even when she posted for Holocaust Remembrance Day, she posted:

> @liceHerShe: Thinking today about all those who were impacted by the Holocaust. The true victims of antisemitism ... Islamophobia, and all other forms of hate.

But @liceHerShe's big break didn't come until the great storm.

Last summer, remnants of Hurricane Lisa swept through the US Gulf States, all the way up through Alabama and into the Tennessee Valley. Hurricane Lisa had not yet been downgraded to a tropical storm; it was still a named hurricane when it hit the Tennessee Valley. Refusing to lose force as the predominantly white male meteorologists predicted would happen as it traveled over land, Hurricane Lisa gained strength, as if to say, *this is my voice, and I won't be silenced.*

As she swept up from Alabama into the Tennessee Valley, her gale force winds overwhelmed the flood-control dams of the Tennessee River System. The destruction and damage left by Hurricane Lisa was immense. When it was over, 300 thousand homes were destroyed and 2,300 lives had been canceled.

As resources to search, rescue, and rebuild the region came in from all over, the world sat in stunned silence. No one knew what to say to those who had lost loved ones or had all their possessions destroyed by the flood. Sorry, to those who had all their possessions destroyed by the storm, not the flood.

@liceHerShe wept as she sat alone in her apartment. She didn't know what to say, so she sat there and cried as she livestreamed her dismay at the destruction from hundreds of miles away. Then she said the only thing that came to her mind. She posted:

> @liceHerShe: Thoughts and prayers to everyone impacted by the storm.

Thoughts … and prayers. No one had ever strung these three words together.

Like, Like, Like, Like, Like!!!! The Internet echoed the ubiquitous approval from all 16 million of @liceHerShe's followers. Like, Like, Like, Like, Like!!! It blew past her followers to new followers, until the resounding shouts of Like!, Like!, Like!, Like! swirled up into gale force winds of their own, this time coming from the north and the west to blow back the flood waters into the banks of the Chickamauga Lake as if to say, *We do not accept your abuse and destruction, it is you who we cancel!*

In a matter of hours @liceHerShe's followers swelled from 16 million to 100 million.

Seeing all the good that was done by those who stood up and rejected the storm, corporations that cared wanted to pitch in. Eschewing their historic focus on profit and share price, corporations cared, not just about shareholders but about all stakeholders. They wanted to show everyone how much they cared and would not stop until everyone in the world could see how much they cared and cared as much as they did, about the same things.

Corporations that cared did away with the old paradigm relationships between company and customer. They no longer sold products to customers; they made retail partnerships where they and their former customers—who were now their partners—could both succeed together. Naturally, companies and customers could only partner with each other if they shared all the same values. Therefore, it was imperative for companies and customers to show they cared about the same things and were alike in every way.

But those in the Tennessee Valley who had lost everything still suffered because they could not feel the "thoughts and prayers" from the rest of the world or see how much their "partner" corporations cared. They could not see any of this because their phones had water damage from the floods. Sorry, water damage from the storm, not the floods.

Apple realized this problem and formed a partnership with @liceHerShe to airlift phones to everyone in the Tennessee Valley who had a water-damaged phone. Unfortunately, those who had purchased insurance on their phones had their policies voided. According to Apple's third-party insurance provider, Hurricane Lisa was a named storm, and named storms were considered Acts of G-d, and insurance did not cover Acts of G-d. Floods on the other hand, were covered under the insurance policy, but the floods did not cause the water damage: the storm did.

Unperturbed by the callous behavior of their third-party insurance provider, who clearly did not care, Apple cared. So, as part of their partnership with @IiceHerShe, they worked out a brand partnership to provide new phones at half price to all their retail partners and potential retail partners in the Tennessee Valley who were impacted by the storm. Furthermore, they set up Apple Pay accounts for each of these partners to allow them to pay off their new half phones in 12 installments, while waiving most of the convenience fees normally associated with setting up the account.

The partnership worked like magic. The world saw how much Apple cared and @IiceHerShe's followers skyrocketed to 250 million.

When the residents of the Tennessee Valley received their new phones, they turned them on and reconnected with loved ones to find out who was still alive and who was canceled. But then, something hateful happened. A selfish element among the residents spoke up. They were ungrateful for all the love and care that was thrust upon them.

The residents of the Tennessee Valley sued Apple for the half-donated phones. They claimed they never agreed to buy them, half price or not. Also, if Apple really cared, they could have their third-party insurance provider, whose name was "Third Party Insurance Provider" and was actually a subsidiary of Apple and not a third party, cover the damage to the phones. And how did the insurance determine that the water damage was caused by the storm and not the flood?

Eager to work with their retail partners, Apple extended their payment terms to an unprecedented 24 months! But that wasn't enough for the ingrates. They said they hadn't wanted the phones and refused to pay for them. When Apple had finally taken enough abuse, they pushed back and said they would have to collect payment within the 24-month window. The ingrates shot back, arrogantly insisting, "We are customers! Isn't the customer always right?" Apple corrected them, noting that the residents were not customers, they were partners, and a partnership meant the residents were only right some of the time, and in this case they were wrong.

Disgusted with the behavior of the ingrates, the search, rescue, and rebuild crews left the Tennessee Valley. The world realized how thoughtless the residents of the Tennessee Valley were, and no longer cared. But @liceHerShe reacted with magnanimity. She sent the message to her followers that she and her brand partner would not react to hate with hate. They would react with love.

That was the last the world thought of the greedy hobbits in the Tennessee Valley. @liceHerShe was awarded a medal by The President, who was really excited to meet her. The whole experience was "so humbling." But more importantly, she had achieved an unprecedented 350 million followers.

———————

The followers, that's who it was all about, @liceHerShe thought as she exhaustedly stepped out onto the dark street after her book signing. The event lasted two hours longer than it was scheduled to, as did every event on the book tour. @liceHerShe refused to end any event until the last of her followers was fully satiated and left of their own free will. The thought of making any of her followers feel rushed left @liceHerShe with an unshakable sense of dread.

If any of her followers felt rushed, they might feel slighted, and to slight a follower was unthinkable. All it took was one slight, or the perception of a slight, or one misplaced comment, or one poorly timed promotion too soon after a national tragedy for any nation in the world, and the dam could break, unleashing an unstoppable cascade of negativity. @liceHerShe had survived that once before and knew she wouldn't be so lucky if it happened again.

Even though she loved her followers, @liceHerShe felt relieved when she left the event that night. She had made it through her book tour without incident and was thankful to have a moment to herself. However, in her state of exhaustion and relief, @liceHerShe had not noticed that the dusk-lit streets that had bristled with the safety of her followers and other pedestrians just an hour earlier had given way to empty sidewalks whose darkness felt more pronounced on this moonless night. By the time @liceHerShe realized how isolated she was, it was too late to go back into the event space. The event staff, *who were the real stars of the night, and had made it all possible*, locked the doors behind her after she left, so they could finally commence cleaning up.

As @liceHerShe pressed on through the dark empty streets, she was on edge, which is why, when a tall, slender, pale man lurched out of the shadows towards her, she wanted to scream and run. However, she fought off her shameful instincts, realizing that, if in fact this was not an attacker, if she ran and screamed and this was just a pedestrian, or even worse, a follower, then this could be the slight that would bring her down.

@liceHerShe stood frozen in silence, using every morsel of willpower she could muster to fight off her flight instinct telling her to run and scream even if it made her a hateful intolerant monster. She held her breath as the shadowy figure outstretched its hand and said, "Ms. Hershe, I am David W. may I speak with you for a moment?"

@liceHerShe breathed a sigh of relief. Her publisher had mentioned that a person named the Davids was looking to meet with her at the event.

"Oh, of course, would you like to take a picture?" @liceHerShe began to purse her lips as she moved to David W.'s side and positioned for a picture.

Without missing a beat, another similarly tall, slender, pale man lurched forward from the same shadow David W. had occupied moments earlier. "Ms. Hershe, thank you, but that won't be necessary. My name is David G. Allow me to get right to the point. Have you ever considered a career in politics? Your views on hatred could really benefit the ticket."

@liceHerShe had never considered politics, but she was flattered and humbled by the question. "I am so flattered. This is so humbling," she responded.

However, as she realized what The Davids were asking, @liceHerShe felt a new panic creep up. She knew the more attention she garnered, the closer the world would come to finding out her dark secret.

The Former President and Natasha
(3.5 YEARS AFTER OPPOSITE DAY DECLARED)

The Former President knew that if he wanted the money from his book deal, he had to answer these boring questions. He had worked out an incredible deal with the publisher. Liberals tried to take his name off everything, but they couldn't take his name off this—it was in his contract. His name would be prominently featured in the title of his authorized biography.

He was now asked to recount the most enduring part of his legacy. The Former President recounted the exact details of how it happened 3.5 years ago.

The Former President sat down. He was livid. How could they call him a racist? He was, like, totally the least racist person he knew, and he knew a lot of racists. He didn't have a racist bone in his body. The brain isn't a bone, right? He loved the Blacks. He loved anyone who liked him and hated everyone who disliked him. Recent polling showed that 90 percent of Black voters disliked him. He hated 95 percent of Blacks.

Blacks turned on him because he had the audacity to merely ask if The Former Former President was born in the U.S. Why was that even racist? Sure, The Former Former President was the first Black person to hold the office, and this was the first time anyone had asked The President this question, but it wasn't like The Former Former President was totally Black, he was half-Black, which to The Former President, meant he had asked this question to the first half-white President.

If anything, why didn't anyone care that he asked this to the white part of The Former Former President? It was like whites had no power anymore. He would have to help restore that; a sense of white power. Restoring white power: that would be an interesting campaign platform for the next election. But Liberals would probably find a way to twist his words and make "white power" seem like a bad thing.

Liberals…they could twist anything. The thought of how they twisted his words burned in his head as he seethed about their duplicity. Also, their hypocrisy, they were like the biggest hypocrites ever. He was so angry now he squeezed his entire body as he clenched down.

At the same time, his stomach churned. It was a Saturday night, which meant he was on his third Chick-Fil-A Spicy Chicken Sandwich of the day. Saturday was his cheat day because it had to be. Chick-Fil-A was closed on Sundays because it was the Lord's Day, which meant The Former President had to load up on sandwiches the day before. He considered an executive order to keep Chick-Fil-A open on Sundays but was advised against it because that could be viewed as attacking the Church, which would play right into the hands of the Liberals.

The Former President wished he hadn't listened to his nerd doctor who advised him to lay off hamburgers. But here he was, eating chicken sandwiches instead of burgers, like a Liberal vegan pussy.

His anger now oozed out of him. The Liberals went too far this time. His smokin' hot wife Natasha told him that Liberal senators were totally talking trash about him behind his back. So, he confronted them.

They said they *weren't,* but he knew they were talking trash, and he would stop it once and for all. He had to control his breathing. He knew once he posted it, there was no going back. But he was ready for it. He pushed and squeezed and squeezed and pushed and pressed and pressed and pressed and pressed! He took out his phone and posted it:

@RealPresident: By executive order, I declare every day going foward to be Opposite Day, and all Americans must adhere to the rules of Opposite Day. [sic]

There were only three rules to Opposite Day:

1. All Americans with different views on any topics were required to completely stop associating with each other.

2. If two people had different views on any issue, they were required to believe the total opposite of the other person's views on all matters.

3. If someone with a different view on any issue did anything, even if not related to the issue in question, assume the worst and hope for their failure.

Opposite Day was the final stop on the train to polarization that the American people had been on for years. The Former President knew this was the nuclear option, and he used it. Having now completed evacuating his bowels, he stood up, took one square of toilet paper, and gave one perfunctory wipe, knowing that he would take a shower in the next few hours anyways, so why bother?

He then looked back into the toilet bowl to inspect his work and screamed into the other room, "Natasha, there's blood in my turds again!"

The Former President then heard Natasha shout back from the other room, "Good, honey, that is a sign of vitality. It is good for you."

Natasha shuddered after shouting back to her husband. This is not how she thought her life would be. However, she saw his post about Opposite Day and took comfort that at least she would now have her vengeance.

Natasha grew up near a Former Soviet country, the kind of former Soviet country that ended with an "ia" and not a "stan". Her husband was very specific with the agency that set them up that she was not to be from a "stan". As a little girl, she dreamed of being beloved. Beloved by her family, beloved by her peers, beloved by people.

It looked like her dreams would come true. She moved to America, married her husband, and was now the First Lady. When she became First Lady, she imagined the people's love would be thrust upon her. The people would fawn over her every move and throw rose petals at her feet.

But no rose petals were forthcoming. Unperturbed, Natasha determined that she would win the affections of the American people the same way she seduced men: by showing them utter indifference.

For years, Natasha thrust her indifference on the American people. However, rather than turning to putty in her hands, they showed indifference back to her. She was perplexed. So, she heaped more indifference on them, and they returned more indifference back to her. She tried every trick she knew; she rolled her eyes, she checked her watch, at every public appearance she looked like she had somewhere better to be. But still, she was unable to crack this war of indifference attrition with the American people. It became physically impossible for her to show them that she had any less desire to be the First Lady.

But the rose petals and adoration of the people still never came. Her hope turned to bitterness. She no longer desired the love of the people; she now wanted them to suffer as she did.

One day, while touring a school, which is where Americans sent their spawn before they are old enough to go to the coal mines or whatever they do here, Natasha came upon a group of girls making fun of a less cool girl. She walked over to the group and asked, "What are you doing?"

The uncool girl fought back tears and replied, "They have called Opposite Day on me, and whatever I do or say, they say the opposite."

Natasha rolled her eyes at the uncool girl, "Thank you so much dear. Can you walk over there before I catch your nerd germs?"

As the uncool girl slumped away, Natasha looked over at the cool girls, "Now, you must tell me what you were doing to that nerd."

One of the cool girls replied, "It's called Opposite Day. Everything she says, we just say the opposite. That way we can be the opposite of that nerd."

Natasha's face then contorted into an unfamiliar position. Her mouth opened, and her lips moved up her face, bunching up her cheeks. She believed this was called smiling. Then she got an idea, an awful idea. Natasha had a wonderful, awful idea.

If the American people refused to love her, then they would love no one, including themselves.

Then, remembering that she was supposed to be at the school to spread a positive message, she turned around to the cool girls and said, "Be best." She then turned, walked away, and slapped the books out of the hands of the uncool girl as she passed by her.

THE DAY
OPPOSITE
DAY
DECLARED

Patricia Ocampo Santos (Me/Me)
(THE DAY OPPOSITE DAY DECLARED)

Patricia Ocampo Santos, or POS as she was affectionately called by her followers, was a third-term congresswoman from New York. She was sent to Washington to represent the under-represented. Brown people, not just Black people, suffered at the hands of a racist system. Patricia couldn't understand how the system could be so structurally racist. She couldn't imagine how some could generalize entire groups of people and hate them all. It made her sick. But not as sick as police made her. She hated all cops. Every single one of them. They were all racist, terrible people.

The system needed to be changed from within, and it was a matter of changing habits. For instance, today was a Tuesday, which historically meant that it was Taco Tuesday in the congressional cafeteria. But Taco Tuesday was a gross oversimplification of Mexico's unique culinary traditions. In order to properly celebrate these traditions, she arranged for chefs to be flown in from different regions of Mexico to prepare more culturally appropriate dishes.

From Northern Mexico they had a chef who specialized in Fajitas, celebrating the rich traditions of Baja California and the different types of flour tortillas found in the region. They had a chef from the Yucatan make conchita pibil in honor of the Mayan influences on Mexican cooking. A chef from Veracruz made pollo encacahuatado to showcase the Afro-Cuban traditions of the region.

23

Some of Patricia's peers complained about the cost of flying in chefs every Tuesday, but there was no price you could put on ending cultural appropriation. So, she took her struggle to change Taco Tuesday straight to the people. She posted:

@POS: Guess the only thing our government won't appropriate is funding to stomp out cultural appropriation in our own congressional cafeteria.

Patricia rose to power in the Liberal Party because she knew how to use the internet, which gave her an advantage over her older peers. A few months before she was elected, the congressional IT person killed himself when a software update disallowed the use of all sequential numerical patterns and the word 'Password' in passwords. This change nullified the most popular password in congress, 'Password1234'. The Deluge of questions, complaints, and threats proved too much for the ill-fated IT person.

The password change caused the operations of congress to grind to a halt. Unbeknownst to the public, about 65 percent of Congress was locked out of their computers for two months. Meetings were missed, Congressional hearings were delayed or canceled, Congress was unable to function on its normal day-to-day basis. But by some miracle, the country was able to carry on as if this had no impact on how the people lived their lives.

Patricia's ability to access and use the internet allowed her to set the agenda for the entire Liberal Party. By the time anyone else in the party read an opposing view, Patricia had already reacted to it. No longer was there a need for parties to craft strategic plans to accommodate the different constituencies they represented. Now, policy was determined by who reacted first. If Washington was the Wild West, Patricia was Billy the Kid.

As Patricia read the statement from The Former President, the cuisines from the different regions of Mexico started to coalesce in her stomach. The foods from the different regions banded together, as if to rise up against the Spanish Conquistador colonial oppressors and avenge their fallen Aztec ruler. She quickly apologized in her head. The Spanish could never have been colonial oppressors, it must have been the English or French somehow. She would have to look it up. Or if not look it up, just post about it. Either way, the forces were coming together, and today Moctezuma would have his revenge.

Luckily for Patricia, other members of Congress, and the executive branch, most policy could now be crafted from the toilet, thanks to smartphones. Patricia pressed down harder and harder as she reached for her phone.

She read The Former President's Opposite Day post. She grinned. This meant she was finally free. No longer could she be held by the shackles of common decency when approaching the other side. She would really go at them now. She squeezed and squeezed and squeezed, but this one was loose and wouldn't require much squeezing, but she did it just for sport.

She typed her response, making sure to send off her message before anyone else responded. This way, it could be the official view of the party. In a stroke of political genius, she knew she could back them into a corner. She posted:

> @POS: We accept The Former President's declaration of Opposite Day... Also, we are concerned for all those impacted by the pandemic.

After she posted, she reached for a handful of 2-ply. She knew that 2-ply was bad for the environment, but she was doing so much good, the world owed her this one small vice. The 2-ply reminded her that she had grown up in a 1-ply household. She was soon in a trance, reaching for handful after handful of 2-ply until she became irritated from over-wiping, which is tough to do with 2-ply. She remembered her childhood, when she went to school, and the rich kids made fun of her because her hands stunk from wiping with the thin sheets of 1-ply in her house. This was the '90s and no one washed their hands back then. But she would never have that problem again.

She left the bathroom without washing her hands, because what was the point of 2-ply if you had to wash your hands? When she stepped into the hall, she looked over to her assistant and said, "I did it again, would you call the plumber and tell them we have another Tuesday situation in the bathroom?"

The Committee to Unify National Tories and Jeffery Tripp Perez

(2 Days After Opposite Day Declared)

Billie and Wilma Davis were the hottest Conservative political consultants. They were young, blonde, and Conservative. Unlike other young Conservatives, they were attractive, so they didn't come off as creepy for being Conservative at a young age.

Being Conservative is more natural at an older age. Still, every grade school has a Conservative kid or two in each cohort. They are often strange, wear ties to school when no uniforms are required and argue with teachers for espousing Liberal views in the classroom. Conversely, Liberals don't age well. Either they get more Conservative with age, when change starts to scare them and threaten the lives they have built for themselves, or they become Conservative through attrition, when the Liberal ideals they held during youth become widely accepted and, therefore, part of the establishment.

Society isn't sure what to do with young Conservatives or old Liberals. They are an imperfection in the algorithm that runs the world. They don't mesh with the overall code, and therefore, they must be isolated so as to not spread their contagion to the rest of the algorithm. As a result, they are sent to pasture in far-off lunch tables in the boondocks of the school cafeteria for Conservative kids, or the state of Vermont for Liberal old people.

But the archetype of Billie and Wilma D. somehow did not disturb this algorithm. They were young, blonde, and attractive. They represented how an older version of the algorithm once defined America. While this was updated in more recent versions of the software, the new software still held a soft spot for them. This allowed them more freedom than other parts of the algorithm, but their code had restrictions they could not violate. If they did, they would draw attention to the glitch in the software that allowed them this freedom and risk a correction in the next version.

Billie and Wilma D. were sisters-in-law. They had married the Davis brothers who were famous for playing football at either the college or professional level. The Davis brothers were non-entities as far as Billie and Wilma D. were concerned. Billie and Wilma D. married the Davis brothers because the Davis brothers were the most efficient conduit to Billie and Wilma D. becoming members of the same family unit. If they were in the same family unit, everyone would know they had the same values and opinions as each other.

They started their political consultancy, the Committee to Unify National Tories, and it quickly became the leading Conservative consultancy in the country. Wilma had a PhD in Applied Mathematics and Economics from MIT, while Billie had a JD/PhD in Law & Political Science from Harvard. However, the website for their consultancy listed their Bachelor's in Kinesiology from State U as their highest level of education. It also mentioned that State U is where they met their future husbands, the Davis brothers, who played Lacrosse or something.

Billie and Wilma D. had two reasons for not mentioning their advanced degrees on their website. The first was that they did not want people to know they studied different subjects in their post-graduate programs. They were always on the same page and never disagreed with each other, which is why they got along and were able to dispatch political advice. They wanted to acquire the knowledge from these programs, and splitting the work was the most efficient way to achieve this. The other reason was that while their code within the algorithm allowed them more freedom in some regards, it also came with some restrictions. If they showed too much intelligence, they would make their clients feel uncomfortable, and this could draw attention to the glitch.

They sat in their office meeting with Jeffery Tripp Perez, the Governor of Florida. Modern day Florida is best described as how Heaven would be if the weirdest religion you could think of turned out to be correct, and the only people who could get in were its most fervent believers. And now, the state was led by this half-wit, Jeffery Tripp Perez. But Billie and Wilma D. needed him, so they would have to wear a shit-eating grin and deal with it.

Jeffery Tripp Perez was born Jeffery Tripp Buckley. As a child, he realized he wanted to go into politics and took the maiden name of his second cousin's wife to better identify with her Cuban heritage. It served him well. The Cuban population in Florida became a major Conservative voting bloc, which eventually helped vault him to the governor's office.

Jeffery walked in 20 minutes late for his meeting. He didn't want to blow this opportunity. He knew that if he was going to be a rising star in the Conservative Party, he needed Billie and Wilma D. on his side.

Jeffery looked up at Billie and Wilma D. as he entered the room and was taken aback. They were stunning. He immediately felt an urge, but the urge was not exactly sexual. He was a rising star, and nothing could interrupt the rise of a star like an affair. Besides, affairs were too unseemly, better suited for common trash. But still, seeing their beauty triggered a biological response within Jeffery. Not to be with either of them sexually, but to be around them platonically. As though being around such beauty and not acting on it was a sort of magnanimity that proved he was a true believer and could not be deterred from his path.

But this was a new world, and an affair required desire from the woman as well. If he could get the sense that one of them desired him and still resist an affair, that would prove his dedication to his path even more. That was the urge that Jeffery felt. He needed to impress Billie and Wilma D.

"Sorry I'm late. I would have been here sooner, but I couldn't find a *cabeza* at the airport. The place is completely empty."

Billie and Wilma D. saw the subtle glance that Jeffery gave them when he entered the room. They had seen the same look countless times before and knew exactly what they were dealing with. Billie and Wilma D. did not need to look at a clock to know that Jeffery was 20 minutes and 17 seconds late. They knew that traveling was challenging due to the pandemic, and Jeffery must have underestimated the variable for delay in his plans. They would not hold it against him. Billie and Wilma D. also knew from context that Jeffery thought *cabeza* meant cab in Spanish, but they chose not to correct him.

Jeffery Continued, "I must admit, I was nervous when you asked me to come up here. This pandemic seems serious, and I just want to make sure I am being super cautious. You know we have never faced anything like this. But I wouldn't worry too much; I think it will be alright. 'This too shall pass.'"

Billie and Wilma D. shuddered at the thought that there was any topic in the universe this moron thought he knew more about than them. But they had been through every other Conservative governor and couldn't find anyone who would go along.

Realizing that they had been silent for too long, Billie D. responded, "Oh my, I love that. 'This too shall pass,' did you come up with that?" She hated herself for placating this child.

Jeffery hesitated momentarily as if he was considering taking credit. Then he said, "No, I can't say I did. But it seems apt. If we hunker down, we can all get through this."

Wilma D. then followed up with, "Well, that's what we wanted to talk to you about. You see, we think of you as a rising star, and want party leadership to look for you to lead the party in the future."

Jeffery had waited a long time to hear that. He tried to make sure his expression remained calm and then asked, "What is it you would like me to do?"

"Nothing. Absolutely nothing," Billie D. replied. "That's the beauty of it. Pretend like there is no pandemic and have your entire state carry on like normal."

Billie and Wilma could tell that Jeffery was choking back fear.

Jeffery looked puzzled, "I don't understand. Is it the economy you are worried about? I'm not sure my state can do much to offset the shutdowns that are occurring everywhere else."

"No, it's not the economy," Wilma D. responded, realizing how irrational Jeffery was. *Why would they worry about the economy if interest rates were low?* "What's important is that POS recently posted that she is concerned about the pandemic. She is a Liberal and a communist. Therefore, you can't have the same concerns as her."

Billie D. continued, "How do you think your Cuban base will view it if you are soft on a Communist? The Liberals lost the Cuban vote when The Former^11 President gave up on the Bay of Pigs. Do you want to give those votes back to the Liberals by going soft on Communism? Do you think you will be a rising star in the party if you lose us our largest foothold in the Hispanic community?"

Jeffery knew this could be his only opportunity to prove he was a rising star. "No, and it's not that I'm scared of the pandemic."

It was clear from his response that not only was he concerned about his career; he also didn't want to look like a chickenshit in front of women he considered attractive.

But then he remembered he had an excuse for being nervous. "It's just that my abuelita, Beatrice Langdon Buckley, lives in the state, and

I've seen what this has done in nursing homes in NYC. That's all. I was just concerned for her sake."

Wilma D. couldn't believe how irrational Jeffery was. His abuelita had little useful life remaining. Shouldn't Jeffery put a lower weighting on her remaining life expectancy than becoming a "rising star"? "Well, if your abuelita can deliver the Cuban vote then we are OK. If not, you have a choice to make."

Later that day, Jeffery walked to a podium where news cameras were set up. He timidly approached the microphones and said in a soft voice:

"There is no evidence that the pandemic poses any outsized risk. I will not enforce any unconstitutional requirements on the state of Florida."

Then he repeated the statement in a louder voice, as if to convince himself.

"There is no evidence that the pandemic poses any outsized risk. I will not enforce any unconstitutional requirements on the state of Florida."

Finally, now that he really believed it, he said it one more time. This time he shouted it loud enough for that New York Commie to hear. He hoped Billie and Wilma D. were watching him and were impressed with his tough decisive action. Either way, he would be brave for them.

"There is no evidence that the pandemic poses any outsized risk. I will not enforce any unconstitutional requirements on the state of Florida."

3.5 YEARS AFTER OPPOSITE DAY DECLARED

Chandra Brown (She/Her)

(3.5 YEARS AFTER OPPOSITE DAY DECLARED)

Chandra Brown looked puzzled at the caller ID as she picked up the phone. "What do you want?" Chandra asked with a mixture of surprise and annoyance.

The Former President knew it would be easy to kill her with kindness, "I just wanted to say that I think you're doing a fabulous job."

Chandra wasn't in the mood for this. Was this a prank call? "Go to Hell, you creep."

The Former President could sense that Chandra had been starved of any sort of affection in the last few months. This would be an easy deal to make. "No, I am being sincere. You know the media is filled with a lot of nasty people, just rotten sad people, and I see them, and they're giving you a hard time, and I just think it's terrible."

Chandra lost herself in the olive branch of commiseration, "Thank you. That's nice of you to say." However, she quickly regained her skepticism, "But what do you want?"

"I mean, what you are doing at the border. Just fabulous, superb work. The chaos you are allowing is making the argument for a border wall better than I ever did," The Former President said without a hint of disingenuity in his voice.

"Is that all you wanted? I'm hanging up," Chandra said, feeling pathetic for being reeled in by what she thought was a compliment.

"Look, Chandra, a lot of people are saying … and I hear it from people I know … fabulous people … they come up to me and tell me they are going to drop you from the ticket," The Former President said.

Chandra reflexively responded with skepticism. "Don't start this. What are you talking about? They couldn't."

The Former President heard her initial incredulity turn into questioning and then concern. "I just wanted to say in case that happened, I think we could make a good team. Think about it, everyone says they hate me, but they secretly like me. Everyone says they like you, but they secretly hate you. Together, we would be perfect."

The idea of teaming up with The Former President repulsed Chandra. "Ugh. That may or may not go against everything I may or may not believe in." Even if he was right, there is no way she would ever take him up on his offer. "It's likely never going to happen, so we don't have to cross that bridge …." But there was no point in fully burning the bridge right now. "At least not right now," she added.

@liceHerShe (She/Her)
(3.5 YEARS AFTER OPPOSITE DAY DECLARED)

liceHerShe joined the ticket as the Liberal candidate for VP a week ago. Things got off to a shaky start. After her announcement as Chandra Brown's replacement, The President's numbers tanked. Supporters were concerned about her lack of experience. The Davids were not worried.

The Davids sat with @liceHerShe to plan her campaign strategy. "Don't worry about it. The people don't know what you stand for yet. Just go out there and post to your followers about your beliefs," David W. assured her.

@liceHerShe couldn't understand how the Davids were so calm. The internet was furious. Did they have ice in their veins? Did they hold nothing sacred? "But before I do, shouldn't we craft a campaign strategy? Shouldn't I coordinate with The President about what to say, what not to say, what issues to highlight?"

"That won't be necessary. Just post about your views." David W. sounded assuring, but @liceHerShe couldn't believe he was so calm. She needed confirmation. She looked over at David G. "David G. do you agree"?

David G. shot back, "Of course I do. Don't be insulting. I just said my thoughts on the matter."

@liceHerShe took her phone and thought for a while. She didn't know anything about creating a national campaign policy. What issues should she address?

She looked back at the Davids one last time to make sure. "OK, so, you just want me to post the cornerstone of my campaign? Do you want me to tell you what it is before I post?"

David G. said calmly, "That won't be necessary. I have full confidence in you."

@liceHerShe was taken aback by the Davids' confidence in her. "Thank you. The support from you two means so much to me."

David W. replied, "Absolutely, you have this. Also, please remember to refer to myself and David using my preferred singular pronoun."

@liceHerShe was horrified. How could she have done that to them? She meant him. Ugh, she felt like such an intolerant monster. "OMG, I am such an intolerant monster. Of course I will."

This teachable moment gave @liceHerShe an idea. She knew what her campaign would be about. She Posted:

> @liceHerShe: "Joining the campaign today as Liberal candidate for VP. In awe of the people around me. My campaign will be about stopping hate."

Reactions to her post were negative. Even her biggest supporters couldn't believe it. She was the candidate for Vice President. She needed a serious issue. This wouldn't do. Within 10 minutes of her post, she lost 30 million followers. 30 million followers!!!

The President called the Davids. @liceHerShe could hear yelling on the other side of the phone. She began to panic. The Davids assured The President not to worry; this was all according to plan. The Davids looked excited when he got off the phone with The President.

David W. looked at @liceHerShe to assure her, "That was perfect. Completely inspired. I knew you could do it."

@liceHerShe couldn't understand how he was so calm. "What are you talking about? People hate it. I haven't had this much online negativity since The Presidents' Day Fiasco." @liceHerShe thought to herself, *The Presidents' Day fiasco. It was all happening again.*

@liceHerShe began hyperventilating. Her doctors said there was a chance her PTSD would come back, especially if she kept her job. But the job was too much a part of who she was, so she continued posting, PTSD or not.

The Presidents' Day fiasco. It all came back to her now.

Three years ago, @liceHerShe was trying to buy a new mattress. She did extensive research on all the brands to make sure she could find the one that had the firmest stance on anti-hatred. She found many mattresses she liked, but each company had a problematic history. Finally, she found the perfect one: Kind Mattress Company. The mattress was truly uncomfortable. It was soft in all the wrong places and felt like it had been used before, but the Kind Mattress Company liked all the right things and supported all the right causes. She contacted them, and after some consideration, they said they would be happy to enter a retail partnership with her. In honor of their new partnership, the partner success associate told @liceHerShe she could save 30 percent if she waited two weeks to buy the mattress, because they were having a Presidents' Day sale.

Presidents' Day, what an ignorant monster she was then. So naïve. 30 percent off, that was the cost of her soul. When @liceHerShe purchased the mattress, she was so pleased that the partner success associate told her about the sale, she posted her appreciation:

> @liceHerShe: "Thanks so much to Kind Mattress Company, my new partners in sleeping. 30 percent off for Presidents' Day. Too good to be true."

The reaction from her followers was justifiably brutal. Presidents' Day!!! How could she engage in such a barbaric holiday? Presidents' Day celebrated the birthdays of The Former^45 President and The

Former^30 President. The Former^45 President owned slaves and there is no need to even go into what The Former^30 President did. Therefore, by buying a mattress from Kind Mattress Company, @liceHerShe was complicit in the slave trade as well as the several unspeakable acts committed by The Former^30 President.

@liceHerShe apologized immediately and attempted to return the mattress. However, by then it was too late.

The banks that had provided the small business loans for Kind Mattress Company faced a backlash of their own. By loaning money to Kind Mattress Company, the banks no longer aligned with the values and beliefs of their other customers. Facing a run on their banks from angry depositors, they called in their loans, forcing Kind Mattress Company to shut its operations and declare bankruptcy.

Ben Kind, the founder of Kind Mattress Company, was financially ruined. But more importantly, his charity was ruined. At Kind Mattress Company, with every mattress that was sold, the company donated one mattress to those in need. The needy accepted the mattresses when they were donated because they didn't want to be rude, but the mattresses were of very poor quality, so they were often thrown out as soon as they were dropped off. Ben Kind was not aware of this, and thought his charity truly provided appreciated goods to those in need.

Devastated that his business and charity were ruined, Ben Kind decided that he would take his life. Ben's life insurance actually covered suicide, so at least his wife and children would get his insurance money and be able to stay in their house.

But Ben Kind turned out to be as ignorant a monster in death as he was in life. One day, when his family was out of the house, Ben Kind got down on his knees and plunged a kitchen knife into his stomach. He was likely aiming for his heart, but he hit his stomach. He bled out on the floor and died shortly after. He didn't have the decency in that time to explain, by writing in his own blood, that he was not aiming for his stomach.

Therefore, his death was as problematic as his penchant for Presidents who owned slaves and did all the terrible things that The Former^30 President had done. Because the knife hit his stomach, the way he killed himself was similar to the Japanese tradition of *seppuku* or honor killing. However, Ben Kind was not Japanese. This meant that he was appropriating the rich culture of sacrificing oneself for honor from the samurai tradition which he had no claim to.

Needless to say, the Internet let Ben Kind's widow and children know about their displeasure. Protests were set up outside of their house. @liceHerShe was dragged into the fallout because of her involvement with the original Presidents' Day Fiasco. Her followers fell from 17 million back to 15.5 million. The internet demanded an apology to the people of Japan, whose culture was so recklessly appropriated by Ben Kind.

@liceHerShe called his widow but was unable to make any headway. The widow would not listen to reason. She said she was too busy with preparations for the funeral to worry about the people of Japan. The widow complained that the insurance company said they would not cover her husband's suicide. Even though suicide was covered in his policy, the insurance company claimed that he was driven to it by depression. Depression was a preexisting condition, and therefore, his insurance policy was nullified.

@liceHerShe saw what a selfish shrew Ben Kind's widow was. *How could she worry about herself at an unprecedented time like this, when Japanese culture was being misappropriated?*

@liceHerShe was left to face the wrath of the people for the actions of an insensitive barbarian. She announced that she was taking a break from all social media and would enter rehab immediately. Her followers were mollified.

Now she was living The Presidents' Day Fiasco all over again, but this time, it was on a much larger and more public scale. Still, she couldn't understand why the Davids didn't seem concerned.

Ted Cruise

(3.5 YEARS AFTER OPPOSITE DAY DECLARED)

@liceHerShe was a spiraling disaster, and Conservatives ate it up. The President took a swing on a dark horse as his running mate and whiffed. Conservatives needed to capitalize quickly. They couldn't let the Liberals back away. They needed Liberals to dig in. @liceHerShe was better than manna from the heavens. She was a Liberal version of a Governor from Alaska.

Ted Cruise was the perfect choice to make Liberals dig in. He was the senior Senator from Texas. He was smart, well prepared for every argument, always a contrarian, smug, arrogant, with a face a mother could drown. Everyone hated him, even Conservatives. But Conservatives voted for him, because even though they hated him, Liberals hated him more. His only appeal to his voters was how much Liberals despised him. Conservatives would use this dynamic to make Liberals dig in for @liceHerShe.

Conservatives sent Ted Cruise on the news circuit to tell everyone what a disaster @liceHerShe was. Hearing Ted Cruise criticize @liceHerShe would make Liberals dig in further, and they would be stuck with a loser candidate.

Citizens had two main sources of news: a Conservative news provider and a Liberal news provider. While both reported the same news, the two sources were able to use different tactics to emphasize and deemphasize different stories depending on the tastes of their viewers. This included giving varying amounts of airtime to different stories, using body language and filler words to highlight the seriousness of a sentence, and most importantly, emphasizing different words to signal the importance or frivolity of a topic.

But when Ted Cruise hit the news circuit, that meant he would go on both Conservative and Liberal news outlets. He first hit the Conservative network. The interview turned out to be a lovefest between Ted Cruise and himself. The anchor asked him what he thought of @liceHerShe's post. He then filled the time answering that question and several follow-up questions he asked himself rhetorically. He had prepared answers to his rhetorical questions for himself, and they were filled with rhetoric.

The mood in the news studio for the Liberal News Network was deflated. They saw what Ted Cruise said during his interview on the Conservative News Network and were prepared for the worst. This would be insufferable. And worst of all, he was right, @liceHerShe was a complete dud of a choice.

Tameika Jordan was the lead producer of the show. She was preparing the anchor for the interview with Ted Cruise when she got a call. She looked at the caller I.D. and decided she should answer it. She excused herself from her meeting with the anchor to take the call.

Tameika answered the phone in a somber tone. It was the Davids. She was surprised she didn't hear any sense of concern in his voice. He had just made one of the largest blunders in the party's history, yet he sounded upbeat. The Davids requested that the anchor maintain control of the interview and not allow Ted Cruise to ask himself rhetorical questions. The Davids also requested that the anchor ask Ted Cruise one simple, straightforward question, which the Davids had prepared himself.

When Tameika heard the question, she laughed as if her eyes were suddenly opened to a hilarious prank. She bit her bottom lip trying to control her laughter, but the chuckles kept coming out. Her somber mood turned into pure glee. This would be fun. But she had to keep the gloomy mood in the newsroom going to better sell the Senator.

She returned to prepping the anchor for the interview. When she told the anchor the question she was to ask, the anchor's face lit up. But Tameika told her to keep it to herself.

Ted Cruise arrived at the elevator to the Liberal News Network studio. He was late because he took time on his way to count cars in the parking lot. He figured he would bring up the fact that the parking lot of the Liberal news network was full, meaning that everyone drove to work. They drove to work even when they preached about how important the environment was, because they were hypocrites.

Ewwww how he hated what big hypocrites Liberals were, it enraged him. During his interview, he would definitely bring up how many cars were in the parking lot. If he brought up how many cars were in the parking lot, then Liberals watching at home would have an epiphany. They would say to themselves, *You know what, this guy is completely right, and I am completely wrong. We are all total hypocrites, and we should switch over and become Conservatives.* Then they would think exactly as he thought and believe in what he believed in, and they would all credit him for their political epiphany, and then he would be voted "Greatest Politician of the Year," the award that had always eluded him, and after his victory speech everyone who had ever picked on him would come up to him and tell him how right he was and how wrong they were.

At this moment, the elevator doors opened, and Ted Cruise realized he was fully erect. After a moment of panic, he realized it wasn't an issue. No one would notice. He had what his doctors called, "a bad dick."

Ted Cruise saw Tameika waiting on the other side of the open elevator door. "Hey, you. I'm late, where do I go for my interview?"

Tameika knew that he knew her name. He had been on their show 30 times in the last five years, and she was the head producer. "Right this way please; we're all set up for you in the studio," Tameika replied doing her best to stay polite. Besides, he looked like he was erect again, and she didn't want to prolong her discussion with him.

Ted Cruise sat down in the studio to be interviewed. Before the interview began, he and the anchor sat in silence, staring at the lights coming from the cameras. At one point, the anchor could swear she heard him saying something to himself. It sounded like the names of different cars. But before she could ask what he was saying, they were being counted in by the production team to go live on air.

The Anchor began the show. "Senator Cruise, thank you for joining us today."

Ted Cruise held back a smirk. "Of course, I wouldn't want to be anywhere else in the world right now."

The Anchor followed up, "The big topic tonight is the post from @liceHerShe earlier. We wanted to get your thoughts."

Ted Cruise let out a breath, as if he had been holding in this answer for about as long as he could bear. "Why, thank you for asking. I thought you never would." The Anchor's question stimulated a half-smirk onto his face. "I have to say that when I heard @liceHerShe was chosen to be the VP on the ticket, I was appalled. It just goes to show what Liberals really feel is important. You don't want someone with substance; you just want someone who says all the right things. I think @liceHerShe is a novice who has no business running for local dog walker, let alone Vice President of the United States."

Ted Cruise knew that "dog walker" wasn't a real elected office, but he was in the mood to be silly. He wanted to show everyone that he could be funny. And then they would know that they were wrong, and he was right.

Ted Cruise then asked his first rhetorical question, "And why was she chosen, you might ask?"

Ted Cruise's half-smirk had now converted to a full-on smirk. "Not because of her credentials or because of her ideas, but because she represents all the awful things that Liberals are jamming down the country's throat." He then asked his second rhetorical question, "When will Liberal voters get sick of this?" The full-on smirk he was sporting began throbbing uncontrollably. "Not soon enough."

After answering his second rhetorical question, Ted Cruise took a breath. The Anchor, who was trying not to stare directly at Ted Cruise's full-on throbbing smirk, seized the opportunity to get in a question. "Senator Cruise, if I may interrupt you. And by the way, thank you for anticipating and answering so many of your own questions. But I was wondering not so much about your thoughts on her post, but her actual message. What do you think of @liceHerShe's view of hating hate?"

Ted Cruise shot the Anchor an incredulous look. He was in full-on throbbing smirk mode. By asking her own question, she was breaking his concentration. He was not the young idealist he once was. It wasn't as easy for him to maintain a full-on throbbing smirk these days. But since she broke his concentration, he knew that if he were unable to give her a fully satisfactory interview, it would not be his fault. No one would look at this situation and say Ted Cruise couldn't maintain a full-on throbbing smirk. They would realize that she distracted him, and there was no problem with Ted Cruise or his smirk. "Honey, I think you need to open your ears. Before you interrupted my questions to myself, I was saying that I think it was stupid."

"Yes, I understand that. What I am asking is, do you agree or disagree with her? Do you want to stop hatred?" The Anchor shot back.

Ted Cruise turned pale. Instinctively, his smirk shriveled away as if it were looking for a hiding place somewhere between his cheeks. He had prepared several snarky answers to all the questions he could think to rhetorically ask himself. But he had not thought about this particular question. He was not prepared to talk about what @liceHerShe actually said.

"You are asking if I want to stop hate?" He stammered this question to the Anchor.

The Anchor held steadfast, "Yes, or are you pro-hate?"

Ted Cruise knew he was trapped. According to the rules of Opposite Day, he had to disagree with whatever @liceHerShe said. If he didn't, he would be a hypocrite and a communist.

"Why, yes, that is what I am saying," he said, sounding like he was questioning his own answer.

The Anchor saw that Ted Cruise was fumbling for an answer. He was likely to take another breath. With the smirk now vanished from his face, the Anchor was free to look directly at him, which made it easier for her to jump in with follow-up questions. "Are there certain types of hate that you support the most? Racial, religious, ethnic?"

Ted Cruise knew @liceHerShe's comment was very general, and therefore he would have to support all hate. "Yes, all those types of hate. I support all those types of hate." The Senator almost whispered the end of his answer. He shrank deeper into his seat by the second.

"How about guns? Do you hate guns?" The anchor could have sworn she saw Ted Cruise mouth, "you fucking bitch" when she asked that question.

Ted Cruise looked down at the ground, "Yes, I hate guns."

The Anchor saw that they were coming to the end of their time for the interview. Despite Ted Cruise not being able to maintain his smirk, she found the interview to be quite pleasurable. "Well, Senator Cruise, not to editorialize, but that's what the news is these days, and I as well as the rest of Liberal America thank you for your support of gun control. Is there anything else you would like to share as we come up on our time?"

By this time, the Senator's smirk realized that there was no place to hide between his cheeks, it was all open space. So, the Senator began to droop in his chair, sinking lower in his seat. Making one last attempt to sit fully erect, he perked up and stammered, "You know…

you… you…you drove a car here." But he was too deflated to finish the thought.

"I'm sorry, I didn't fully understand that," the anchor added in a conciliatory tone. "We will have to hear more about that next time."

The Davids (1/1)

(3.5 YEARS AFTER OPPOSITE DAY DECLARED)

The Davids were on his way back from meeting with @liceHerShe when he got the third call from a number he had ignored all night. Now that he weren't with @liceHerShe, he would have to pick up the call.

As soon as the Davids picked up the call, Patricia Ocampo Santos got right to business. "I don't get it; you say I am the rising star in the party and then you give the VP spot to some Karen who has no experience. You are making her look too good."

David W. lightly chuckled, to give Patricia the sense that her concerns were unfounded. "Patricia, what are you talking about? People don't like her. Did you see the reactions? They just hated what she makes others say even more. Don't you get it?"

"But look, she already regained half the followers that she lost. How is that even possible?" Patricia shot back.

David W. broke with his attempt to laugh off her concerns and snarled, "Don't be stupid, we have been buying her followers for some time now. Half of them are Russian robots."

David G. continued, "She will not come out of this looking good. We needed a novice who can tank her popularity while taking down Conservatives as well. Trust me, if you play everything right, you will be there to swoop in. You don't want her job now."

Patricia was somewhat appeased by the explanation, but she didn't want the Davids to think she trusted him. "That better be the case. I know where the bodies are buried. Remember I know what you did to the IT guy."

David W. would not take the bait and lose his temper. He wanted to show Patricia that he and David G. had ice in his veins. "You mean, what we did to the IT guy. And I don't use the word "we" lightly."

David G. shuddered at his use of the *W* word, but continued, "But you're right, you are the future. And if you are the future of the party, you need a stronger staff. I am sending you my top person. He's a lawyer, but he will serve as your aide. His name is Rory Cohen."

Patricia snapped back, "Cohen? A lawyer named Cohen. You know I hate …"

But before she could finish, David W. interrupted, "Don't worry, he is J street."

Patricia sighed in relief, "Oh, OK. Why didn't you just say that? I was worried. Back to this @liceHerShe. When do we tell her what we have on her?"

David G. replied, "Don't be a fool. This is not the right time for that. You need to have patience."

Rory Cohen (It/It)

(3.5 YEARS AFTER OPPOSITE DAY DECLARED)

Rory Cohen was a righteous man, blameless in his generation. He was an old soul who never identified with the time period in which he lived. This made him an outcast, so he traveled the world, searching for his place. When he could not find his place in the modern world, he looked to the past to find a period in history that felt more like home. When he found periods in history that felt more like home, he realized he could not physically go. He blamed a higher power for assigning his life to a period of history that did not suit him. Rory channeled his disdain for that higher power through the religion of his upbringing. He was raised Jewish but converted to self-hating Judaism shortly after his Bar Mitzvah.

As a proponent of Jewish stereotypes, Rory became a lawyer. He became a world-class lawyer—not a typical ambulance chaser who did personal injury cases. He was too good for that. Rory was the kind of lawyer who defended mothers who killed their children. *Allegedly* killed their children.

He did most of those cases pro-bono to raise his profile. He always won. Many times, his defendants would add horrific crimes on top of what they had done to attract him on a pro-bono basis. The more horrific the crime, the higher the profile of the case. The higher the profile of the case, the more likely Rory was to take the case and win.

Rory became affiliated with the Liberal Party after representing two of The Former^11 President's cousins in the suspicious deaths of two young women. This was not one case involving both cousins and two dead young women. These were two separate cases, wholly unrelated to each other, where each cousin was involved in the suspicious death of a young woman. Women should be careful around this family. Women flocked to them. Being around this family was like living in Camelot, because people had the same life expectancy as if it were England in 500 A.D. This was a time period in which Rory felt at home.

Rory felt so at home that he left his law practice, which was financially floundering due to all his pro-bono cases, to join the Liberal Party full-time.

Now the Davids told him to go work for Patricia Ocampo Santos. Neither Rory nor POS knew it, but before their time together was over, they would bring back a sense of justice not seen since the Dark Ages.

110 YEARS BEFORE OPPOSITE DAY DECLARED

James Bennet

James Bennet's family settled in Tulsa, Oklahoma. They chose Tulsa because it was home to the most thriving Black community in the country. The district of Greenwood was called "the Black Wall Street." Wall Street was an exaggeration. The community was better off than other Black communities, but it was still far from the standards of a white middle-class neighborhood.

Still, the Black community of Tulsa was on the ascent. It was self-sufficient. Businesses were owned by Blacks. Doctors in the community were Black. The government was white.

Charles Roan

Charles Roan was excited to move to Tulsa. He and his family had lived in the neighboring Osage County his entire life, but they finally got permission from their guardian, Mr. Hale, to move to the city.

He knew what the government and all the newspapers said. The Osage weren't wise enough to think for themselves. They would blow through their money just as quickly as they came into it. That's why every Osage who owned rights to land with oil was legally required to appoint a white guardian to oversee their finances. Charles didn't know why his parents seemed to hate the guardian rule. Charles thought they were lucky to have Mr. Hale. Mr. Hale wasn't a stranger. He was a family friend and longtime neighbor.

Anyways, they would prove all the papers wrong. The first thing his parents did when oil was found on their land was to arrange for him and his sisters to attend the best schools. They were all at the top of their classes, except for Lucy. Charles' parents always worried about her.

Thinking about Lucy only upset Charles. They had to delay their move to Tulsa by two weeks because she was missing again. No one was too worried; she was always doing stuff like that. When they decided to go ahead with the move, his mother said chances were, she would show up a few counties away when she and whatever new boyfriend blew through the money she had on her.

Charles knew Lucy was an embarrassment. He could tell his parents thought that it was Osage like her that made the outside world think all Osages needed guardians in the first place.

3.5 YEARS AFTER OPPOSITE DAY DECLARED

The Committee to Unify National Tories

(3.5 YEARS AFTER OPPOSITE DAY DECLARED)

Billie and Wilma D. needed to stop the hemorrhaging. This was a disaster. @liceHerShe seemed like a political lightweight, and she was, but they had never seen a politician so willing to sacrifice themselves to take down the other side. Her behavior seemed like a corruption in the system.

With every post, whatever was left of @liceHerShe's popularity plummeted. Her comments were so vacuous that they warranted no response. But whenever the media asked a Conservative politician what they thought of her comments, their answers alienated voters.

If everyone hated @liceHerShe's comments, then how could they also hate when Conservatives said the opposite? This made no sense, if @liceHerShe was wrong, then wasn't the opposite of what she said naturally correct?

Billie and Wilma D. considered a media blackout after the Senator Cruise incident, but that was not feasible in an election year. He was one of their most experienced members, and he was left so dumbfounded that he had been unable to formulate his point about cars in the Liberal parking lots. After the interview, Senator Cruise was left as a shell of his former self. He walked around the halls of Congress in a zombie-like state, mumbling the names of different cars to himself.

The point about the Liberal parking lot that Billie and Wilma instructed Ted Cruise to use was pure gold. How could a Liberal care about the environment and drive a car to work? Cars were bad for the environment. That behavior contradicted a concern for the environment. How could Liberals reconcile this logical inconsistency? It's what their clients called Liberal hypocrisy.

Billie and Wilma D.'s clients frequently spoke about the hypocrisy of the other side. Sometimes they talked about it with unbridled glee, other times with insatiable anger. Billie and Wilma D. detected one of those two emotions every time a client spoke about hypocrisy. It was peculiar how the same accusation could bring about such contradictory emotions from the accuser on such a consistent basis.

Billie and Wilma D. needed to stop @liceHerShe from taking down Conservative politicians. Her anti-hate post that took down Senator Cruise was just the beginning. Her post supporting the troops took down a Utah congressman. A Georgia senator faced backlash after her post about violence against women. The country barely avoided an international incident after she wished the Prime Minister of Japan a speedy recovery following an emergency appendectomy.

At least their calculations on the primary were correct. The Former President defeated Jeffery Tripp Perez just as they wanted. Jeffery Tripp Perez was their rising star, but this was not the right time for him. The Former President would not go quietly, and Billie and Wilma did not want to risk splitting the ticket if The Former President lost the primary and then ran as a third-party candidate.

Furthermore, they would prefer for Jeffery to run in the next election rather than try to unseat an incumbent. Either way, they had brokered a deal for Jeffery to be The Former President's VP running mate.

The Former President's age, weight, diet, and list of enemies made the role of Vice President a desirable position. Historical data showed that a Vice President had a 13.79 percent chance of taking over due to the death of an elected president. Overlaying this probability with the latest actuarial tables for The Former President's age and weight took that likelihood up to 32.57 percent. Add to that the likelihood of The Former President being removed from office due to impeachment, and subtract his willingness to leave office after impeachment, and the likelihood of his Vice President becoming president increased to 40.17 percent.

While The Former President as the Conservative candidate was the outcome they had predicted, his volatile nature introduced many unpredictable variables into the equation. However, they were working from behind, so adding random variables into the election wasn't necessarily a bad thing.

Owen Cosgrove

It was the best of the worst times, it was the worst of the best times. Times were mediocre. Mediocre didn't sell newspapers. Liberal hypocrisy and social injustice sold newspapers. No one bought newspapers, everyone got their news for free. The Fourth Estate had to work harder to sell newspapers. The Fourth Estate wasn't worried about selling newspapers -- while corporations cared, the Fourth Estate cared more. They thought as their supporters thought and believed in what their supporters believed in; but in order to keep doing that, they needed to keep the lights on. They needed to keep the lights on because they moved to a 24-hour news format. The lights never went off, the news never stopped. Even if there was nothing to report, there needed to be news.

There were two types of people to whom the 24-hour news format appealed. The Liberal News Channel appealed to travelers stuck at airports. The Liberal News Channel was played on TVs at airports and relied heavily on the support of delayed travelers everywhere. While the Liberal News Channel depended on the support of the mobile who were temporarily immobile, the Conservative News Channel depended on the support of the immobile, who would never again be mobile: the elderly who could no longer travel.

Owen Cosgrove was a journalist at the Conservative News Network. For the first time in a while, he was excited about a story.

Initially, after Opposite Day, Owen wrote the stories that sold the news, and had some fun with it, but he was tired of that.

Owen went into his editor's office just as his editor was finishing up his previous call.

"H-Y-P-O-C-R-I-S-Y!!!" The editor shouted into the phone and hung up the receiver. "Sorry, I was just finishing my last meeting. What you got for me?"

Owen sat down on the other side of the editor's desk, "Well, this is exciting. I was contacted by a source at the White House, and ...."

The editor stopped Owen before he could finish, "Who, Chandra Brown? She's been calling everyone. What's the big deal?"

It was Chandra Brown, but Owen couldn't disclose that, no matter how obvious it was. "My source at the White House says The President is acting strangely." Owen continued, "He's been ducking out of meetings to take calls on his cell phone. He's been very secretive about these calls."

"Let me guess," the editor said with a patronizing tone, "You want to take a few weeks, do some research, and write a story on it."

"Well, I think it could be something big. I need at most a week or two." Owen said, in an almost pleading manner.

The editor fell back in his chair. "A week or two, are you crazy!?!? Look out there. What do you see? I'll tell you what you see. It's a bullpen of reporters hungrier than you, getting stories that people care about more than yours." The editor was now yelling more than normal, "For instance, there is an environmental conference on the West Coast this week. Do you know what that means?"

Owen sighed. He knew what that meant.

The editor continued without waiting for Owen's response. "I'll tell you what it means. It means, all these limousine Liberals will fly privately to the conference. Do you know what that is?"

Owen tried to break in, "Yeah, I know, but..." Owen knew the editor wouldn't let him respond. Of all the subjects that got the editor worked up, this one really stood out.

"It's hypocrisy!!!! Elitist, Liberal H-Y-P-O-C-R-I-S-Y!!! That is the news story people care about, they tune in for, they even buy papers for. Do you know what else is happening this week?"

Owen knew he wouldn't be able to get into the conversation before the editor responded to his own question. "College students at an elitist Northeast university signed a petition to get a teaching assistant removed from a class for referring to students without first asking their pronouns. Do you know what that is?"

Owen tried to break in with a response, but he knew what was coming. "Yeah, I realize, but…"

The editor frantically waved his arms as he spoke. Of all the topics that got the editor excited, there was only one topic that drove him into this sort of frenzy.

"CANCEL CULTURE!!!" the editor shouted. "We are under attack, and our viewers need to know about it. You've been through this before. During a time of war, your sissy human-interest stories just don't make the cut."

"You know what else is happening this week?" The editor was becoming more incensed. "The Chicago City Council is trying to fire a police lieutenant for putting a camera in the women's bathroom. You know what that is?"

Owen glanced at the editor with his eyebrows raised, "Boss, that seems pretty bad."

The editor sat forward in his chair and was quiet for a moment. It looked to Owen as if the editor was thinking about something. "Yeah, you know, I realized that when I said it out loud. One second." The editor pressed the intercom button on his desk.

The editor then yelled into the intercom, "Tell Jacobs to scrap that Chicago story ASAP. Also call HR and tell them to look into Jacobs. He could be a perv."

The editor turned back to Owen. Owen knew he had one chance to break in. He wasn't going to win this one with the facts. He had to sell the story.

Before the editor could remember what he was previously shouting about, Owen jumped into the conversation. "Just let me finish. You didn't let me tell you who I think the calls are from."

The editor regained his senses, "I don't care if they're from Osama bin Laden's mother, you've already lost my interest."

Without waiting for the editor to finish his sentence, Owen shouted, "I have reason to believe that the calls are from the Woke Mafia."

The editor fell back in his chair waving his arms even more frantically now. Owen knew that of all the people that angered the editor, no one did so more than the Woke Mafia.

The editor jumped to his feet, "Really?! The Woke Mafia?! We've been after them for years. I knew this guy was dirty. OK, you have your two weeks. Get those SOBs!"

With that, Owen stood up and said, "Thanks, chief. I will," and left the editor's office as quickly as possible.

Owen set off looking into the calls. He didn't know who they were from, but it better be interesting. If he came back with nothing, he would likely lose his job.

4.0 YEARS AFTER OPPOSITE DAY DECLARED

Jeffery Tripp Perez

(4.0 YEARS AFTER OPPOSITE DAY DECLARED)

It had been a sad week, but Jeffery Tripp Perez felt comforted when he saw his entire family gathered together. They had come together on this occasion for the funeral of Jeffery's abuelita.

During the service, Jeffery could sense that his hermano, Preston Archer Buckley, was giving him the cold shoulder. In fact, he sensed that members of his family blamed him for the death of his abuelita. But he wasn't to blame.

His abuelita did not die from the new Alpha-Alpha strain of the pandemic. She had gone to the hospital for a routine hip replacement surgery and died after contracting an infection. Before the surgery, Jeffery's family pleaded with him to allow the surgeon to wear a mask, but it was too hypocritical of him to allow doctors to wear masks when treating his family while he enforced a mask ban at all hospitals throughout the state.

Jeffery conferred with several scientists and doctors of theology and found that not only did masks provide no help against the Alpha-Alpha strain, they were also useless in the daily lives of doctors. Allowing doctors to wear masks robbed people of the natural immunities they would gain from sharing germs on a normal daily basis. Therefore, he banned all mask wearing at all hospitals in the state. If the surgeon couldn't figure out that he was sick before the surgery, then he shouldn't be a doctor.

His family didn't even check in on him after he lost his primary to The Former President. None of them believed he would win. But he did not want to win that race. It was not why he was there.

Before the primary, Billie and Wilma had convinced Jeffery that he should allow The Former President to win the Conservative nomination. They believed that The Former President would run as a third-Party candidate if he lost the Primary, and then Jeffery would then be faced with a split Conservative ticket against an incumbent Liberal.

Also, by going along with The Former President, Jeffery could prove his loyalty to the most important faction of the Conservative Party, the Conservative Conservatives. Once he proved his loyalty to the Conservative Conservatives, Jeffery would be unstoppable in his next election.

The Former President

The Former President knew who he would pick for VP. Everyone called him a racist. But he wasn't a racist. They said he hated the Blacks and he hated the Mexicans, but he didn't. They disliked him, so he hated them back. That's it, they started it, end of discussion. In fact, there was only one group that The Former President hated: fat people. He couldn't stand fat people. They were just so…sloppy! He hated sloppy!

His critics called him fat, which by the way, was totally unfair. He wasn't fat. He was 76. You can't be fat at the age of 76. If you die from a heart attack at 76, no one says it's because you were fat, it's because you were 76. Plus, there was a difference between being fat at 76 and being fat at 40.

He didn't know if he was fat when he was 40. He wore a tuxedo every day from the ages of 30 to 60, and those are very slimming. The only time he took off his tux back then was to be fitted for a new tux. And his tailor, who by the way was Black or possibly Italian, never said he was fat.

But now he would prove that he didn't hate the Blacks once and for all, by showing the world that he could sort of tolerate one of them. He posted:

@RealFormerPresident: "Welcome, Chandra Brown, to the ticket as candidate for VP. Now the Blacks know the truth … I love'em."

The Committee to Unify National Tories

(4.0 YEARS AFTER OPPOSITE DAY DECLARED)

Billie and Wilma D. double-checked the Former President's choice for Vice Presidential candidate. This had not been in their calculations.

However, the good thing about The Former President is that Billie and Wilma would not have to do damage control on the second part of his post. Everyone would only focus on his choice for Vice President.

The Former President's ability to make these comments followed the laws of the algorithm. Voters in a democracy had a sixth sense for how likely a politician was to apologize, and if there was any possibility of a politician apologizing, then that politician was dead in the water. The number one rule in politics wasn't, "don't apologize," it was, "don't look like you would ever apologize."

A politician who apologizes opens the floodgates to criticism from the other side. The other side won't stop at an apology. Demands for an apology are a Trojan Horse. The Greeks didn't storm Troy to get Helen back; they were there to sack the city.

While The Former President's choice for VP was unexpected, it did have its merits. Also, his post gave them an idea. They knew how they would handle the @liceHerShe problem.

Before they did anything, they needed to get the message to Chandra Brown: don't respond to any media questions. Of all the people in the world, she did not have the political capital to survive an @liceHerShe statement.

Chandra Brown

(4.0 YEARS AFTER OPPOSITE DAY DECLARED)

Chandra Brown shuddered when she saw The Former President's post. She knew she was being used. She didn't have any misconceptions about that, but did it have to be so obvious? This hurt, but it was expected. What really hurt was how Liberals used her. She was more than qualified for the role and smart enough to do the job, so why didn't anyone want her?

To be fair, she was using Conservatives as much as they were using her. This was just another deal to advance, or in this case, stay in the game. But it would all pay off when she was president. Then she could … wait, why did she want to become president? She hadn't thought about that question in a very long time.

She began searching her memory for the thread of reasoning she once had used to drive her to seek power. But the thread led to a Gordian Knot of deals and compromises she had made along the way to gain power or raise her profile. She approached her career by collecting all the right jobs. But each job was just a stop along the way. There was no time to leave her mark. From the prosecutor's office to the state's attorney general to the Senate. At the time, she felt like she was moving up, like she was a rising star. But she focused on moving up the entire way at the cost of her current jobs. She performed competently most of the time, but she never invested herself in the present, and this weighed on her results.

On paper, she had all the right attributes. Why couldn't America just love her like they were supposed to? Then she remembered: It was that racist 3rd grade teacher who said she would never be anything. That's why she wanted power. She would show that myopic bitch.

Ted Cruise

Audi 80, Audi 90, Audi A3, Audi A4, Audi R8, Audi A1, Audi A2, BMW 326, BMW 328, BMW 327, BMW 503, BMW 507, BMW 3200 CS, BMW 2000C, BMW i3, BMW i8, BMW M1, BMW 3 Series, BMW 5 Series, BMW 8 Series, BMW X5, Bugatti 18, Bugatti 30, Bugatti 35, Bugatti 37, Bugatti 38, Bugatti 39 ....

99.0 YEARS BEFORE OPPOSITE DAY DECLARED

James Bennet

Rubble and char were all that was left. The pharmacy James Bennet's family owned was burned to the ground. Every business and nearly every building in the Greenwood section of Tulsa had burned to the ground. James was lucky to be alive—nearly 300 members of the community had been killed in the violence a month prior.

James saw a letter from the insurance company. They had denied the claim. His family had fire insurance, but the insurance didn't cover damage from a riot. No one had riot insurance. No one could rebuild.

"The Tulsa Race Riot," that's what they called it. But it felt more like a massacre than a riot. The night before the violence, Blacks in the community armed themselves to protect a Black suspect in police custody from being lynched by an armed white mob. The armed white mob would not submit to mob rule from another mob, so they got government-issued weapons. When the armed Black mob retreated, the white mob sacked Greenwood.

Charles Roan

The ringing in Charles Roan's ears had become all too familiar. It was the sound he heard every time he was told that a family member had died. The only consolation was that this time would be the last time he heard the ringing. There was no one left.

It all began when Lucy turned up dead. It was tragic, but not too surprising. With her lifestyle, it just made sense. But over the next seven years, Charles' parents died in a gas explosion at their house, and two of his sisters died from liver disease. The coroner and the papers too quickly jumped to alcohol, and no one had a problem believing that another Osage drank themselves to death, but it all made no sense to Charles. They didn't even drink. Now his youngest sister Ruby had been found, shot in the woods.

The grief had become too much for Charles, and under the guidance of Mr. Hale, he gave up on living in Tulsa and moved back to Osage County. Mr. Hale took a more forceful role as financial guardian and was now solely in charge of all business decisions.

4.5 YEARS AFTER OPPOSITE DAY DECLARED

@liceHerShe (She/Her)
(4.5 YEARS AFTER OPPOSITE DAY DECLARED)

@liceHerShe was having fun. Not wanting to allow the chance for her PTSD to come back, the Davids put her on a strict media blackout. She was allowed to post, but she was not allowed to look at any reactions to her posts.

She felt so blessed to have the Davids looking out for her. She couldn't believe that just over a year ago she thought he were creepy. He had turned out to be her rock. She felt bad for judging the Davids so quickly back then. She wanted to do something to honor what a good friend he had become. She posted:

> @liceHerShe: "Thinking about a friend today. Just goes to show you: Don't judge a book by its cover."

The Former President

The Former President listened to Billie and Wilma D.'s advice. He waited for a post from @liceHerShe. He was going to put this to bed right now. He posted

> @RealFormerPresident: "I know who @liceHerShe is talking about. They are total freakshows. Sick of Liberals acting as weird as they can. If anything, we need to start judging more books by their covers."

The Davids (I/I)

(4.5 YEARS AFTER OPPOSITE DAY DECLARED)

The Former President's post set off a firestorm. Conservatives who were afraid of the @liceHerShe trap saw it as a rallying cry. General statements wouldn't be enough to box them in anymore. The shame that Liberals depended on to keep Conservatives in check did not apply to The Former President. Now that their leader was unable to be shamed, Conservatives could drape themselves in the cloak of shamelessness.

The Davids could see that he had overplayed his hand. It was stupid of him to think that @liceHerShe could continue to keep all Conservatives muzzled. She had served her purpose until now, but she would be useless from here.

Liberals were on the ropes. This couldn't have come at a worse time. Thanks to @liceHerShe silencing the opposition, Liberals were heading into the final stretch of the campaign with a significant lead. But they had lost steam in the last few weeks.

Conservative news outlets complained that The President was too old and too aloof for the job. They had repeated this charge during every newscast over the last three years, but this time, they tried a novel approach: they used actual journalism to make their point.

The Davids knew that if The President were going to survive this, he would need the help of a rising star.

Owen Cosgrove

(4.5 YEARS AFTER OPPOSITE DAY DECLARED)

It had been months since Owen's editor gave him two weeks to investigate The President's phone calls. Owen had gotten hold of The President's phone records and found that The President spent an average of two hours a day on his personal cell phone. That seemed like a lot. But what was stranger was the lack of consistency in the numbers that called him. The calls came from a wide variety of area codes; some were even 800 numbers. What many of the numbers had in common was that they ended in 000, like 3000, 5000, 6000. It was as though The President was taking calls from the main switchboards of businesses.

Owen researched the numbers. Many of them belonged to different shell corporations. Was his editor right? Was The President dirty? He didn't seem like it. Some of those around him did, but not him. Or probably not him. It was hard to tell what The President had been like when he was younger.

Owen investigated each of the businesses that called The President. These were not outside business interests The President was speaking with. The President was taking calls from telemarketers and pyramid schemes.

The allegations were made more damning when a former White House source, Chandra, corroborated Owen's story and gave an anecdote of how The President almost put a reverse mortgage on the White House. Further, The President's Social Security number turned up after a cursory dark web scrape. This was a national embarrassment and one of the largest security breaches in the country's history.

When Owen brought the story to his editor, the editor looked deflated.

The editor sat back in his chair, uncharacteristically neither yelling nor waving his arms. "You're telling me that the Woke Mafia is not involved?"

Owen knew the editor had his heart set on nailing the Woke Mafia, but he had to understand the importance of the story. "No, but you understand the national security implications, right?"

The editor sighed, "Yeah, I do. I guess we'll have to run it. But why can't you be more like Jacobs? He just brought me a story about how the Woke Mafia was canceling a congressman for trying to coerce a college intern into sex."

Owen raised his eyebrows and looked at the editor. "Boss?"

The editor sat forward in his chair and was quiet for a moment. Owen could tell he was thinking about something. "Yeah, I just heard it when I said it. I need to fire that guy. He's just so convincing."

Owen's story led the news that day for 12 hours until it was bumped from the top spot when a Conservative blogger posted a weekly story about urban decay in both New York and Los Angeles.

Chandra Brown

Chandra Brown was coming into her own. As it turned out, she loved being Conservative. Much like when she was a Liberal, she believed in about 50 percent of the positions she took. But this time, people loved her for it.

Chandra finally felt she was on the right path. Instead of worrying about the next opportunity, she would do her best where she was. Advancement would take care of itself. Her star was fading in the Liberal Party, but she was a rising star in the Conservative Party. Conservatives had no concern that she had switched parties. Most Conservatives were at one time Liberal: so, to them, switching was just the natural progression of life. They welcomed her with open arms.

She had finally found a home. She was never going back.

Jeffery Tripp Perez

(4.5 YEARS AFTER OPPOSITE DAY DECLARED)

Jeffery Tripp Perez groaned when he saw The Former President's post. He was on the outside looking in, and with only one month until the election, Jeffery needed to find a way to make himself relevant again on the national stage again. Ever since he was passed over for Vice President, his star had remained stagnant. Rising stars needed to rise, if they ceased rising, they would fall. It was basic astronomy. Aside from that, Jeffery was not having a good week. The Supreme Court had overruled his ban on masks in hospitals, even though they were supposed to be on his side.

Liberals claimed that the new Alpha-Alpha strain of the pandemic was gaining strength in Florida. Jeffery conferred with his council of doctors, who confirmed that the Alpha-Alpha strain was Liberal propaganda. That was the exact phrasing from the doctor of applied mathematics on the council.

There were Judases everywhere. Jeffery had to fire his longtime chief of staff for allowing his children to trick-or-treat in Ninja-Turtle costumes that had masks. He gave strict instructions to all state employees that the no-mask mandate had to be followed with the strictest adherence. If anyone were to break it, it would make them just as hypocritical as Liberals. Liberal hypocrisy. He just learned the meaning of this phrase and was still getting the hang of it.

To make matters worse, his childhood friend and longtime donor, Buxton Conrad Bancroft, died from a mysterious respiratory infection. Jeffery got the sense that Buxton's family blamed him for Buxton's death, but they were too averse to confrontation to say anything at the funeral.

Those Liberal freakshows, the Davids, showed up at the funeral. They are real creeps. They came with umbrellas to shield themselves from the sun. It was quite the spectacle. Jeffery wasn't sure why they were there. The Bancrofts were desperate to avoid a scene and didn't say anything.

Jeffery took it upon himself to approach the Davids. Jeffery knew that this interaction was fraught with danger. If the Davids made a scene, not only would Jeffery be scandalized, but it could also impact the rise of his star in the Conservative Party.

Jeffery approached the Davids with an intense feeling of trepidation, "Gentlemen, can I help you?" Jeffery looked at the Davids to see if his use of the plural of gentleman had stung them.

The Davids looked unaffected by Jeffery's slight, or at least were unwilling to give Jeffery the satisfaction of showing any hint of emotion. "Good afternoon, Governor Buckley, I just stopped by to offer my condolences," David W. said as he smirked.

Unlike the Davids, Jeffery was unable to keep the emotions off his face and gave a brief look of aghast surprise when David W. addressed him by his birth surname. Jeffery could not believe the Davids had the audacity to call him by a name he no longer identified with. *How could they be so thoughtless and cruel?* Jeffery thought to himself. *Or was it "he" be so thoughtless and cruel? Ugh, they were such weirdos, who cared what they made everyone call them?*

"Thank you both for your condolences. Buxton was a good man. I wasn't aware that either of you knew him," Jeffery saw that the Davids were still smirking. He was no longer sure if they were smirking because of the subtle dig they had taken at him, or if they just enjoyed being at a funeral.

"We had met him in passing a few years ago. We were in the neighborhood and didn't want to miss the opportunity … " David G. oddly paused before finishing, "to pay our respects of course."

Then David W. put out his hand and said, "We must be on our way now."

Jeffery would have normally scoffed at shaking hands with either of these freaks, but he was desperate for the interaction to end without incident, and readily took David W.'s hand.

When David W. clasped Jeffery's hand, instead of offering a salutation, David W. looked deeply into his eyes repeating the phrase, "Remember your friend."

Jeffery was saddened by the death of his friend. He remembered their time as young adolescents, friendly competitors in many of the sports that young teens play: tennis, golf, skeet shooting, and dressage. Buxton was the more natural dressage performer. He looked effortless as the horse performed its moves, such as trotting and turning around.

He also remembered times before their adolescence that were more carefree and less buttoned up. Jeffery hadn't thought about those times in years. He still went by Buckley back then. He and Buxton would run in the woods and make forts near the trees. They built a clubhouse that required a secret handshake to enter, which only they knew. That gave Jeffery an idea. He could use that handshake to simultaneously remember his friend and sniff out traitors in the Conservative Party.

Jeffery then realized that he and David W. were still shaking hands as David W. looked into his eyes and repeated, "remember your friend." *What freakshows these guys were,* Jeffery thought as he pulled his hand away. As the Davids turned away and left the funeral, Jeffery knew exactly what he would do.

After the funeral, Jeffery called a press conference. He would not have Billie or Wilma D. check with party leadership on this. He was his own man, a rising star in the party, and he would both take initiative and remember his friend.

At his press conference, Jeffery called up his new chief of staff, who looked reluctant to be there, likely because it was his first time in front of the cameras. Jeffery then announced to the room of reporters, "I have a new handshake for Conservatives and only Conservatives. If you think as I think and believe in what I believe in, you should use this and only this handshake."

The new chief of staff was now openly cringing. Jeffery then spat into his hand and waited for the new chief of staff to spit into his own hand. Then the two then shook hands, combining their spit and becoming spit brothers. As they shook hands and the cameras snapped pictures, Jeffery thought to himself, *this one's for Buxton.*

The new handshake was wildly successful, and its success was not confined to Florida. The Spit Brothers' Handshake became instantly prevalent in Conservative enclaves throughout the country. In some heavily Conservative areas, they skipped the handshake and just spat directly into each other's mouths, although they made sure to say "not in a gay way" each time. Homosexual advocacy groups went back and forth about releasing a statement condemning the assertion that homosexuality had anything to do with the desire to spit in someone's mouth, or have someone spit in your mouth, but decided to remain silent on the subject so as not to interrupt Conservatives from spitting in each other's mouths during a pandemic.

Jeffery Tripp Perez watched with pride. He had started a movement that Conservatives were supporting on a national scale. This would solidify his role as a rising star. He thought of Billie and Wilma D. and how impressed they must be.

The Committee to Unify National Tories
(4.5 YEARS AFTER OPPOSITE DAY DECLARED)

That limp dick halfwit. Billie and Wilma D. knew Jeffery was stupid, but they didn't think he would knowingly spread the Alpha-Alpha strain to his own support base heading into the election. Before the Spit Brothers handshake, the pandemic was waning and on its last legs. The Alpha-Alpha strain was a relatively benign mutation, but Jeffery spread the strain with such efficiency that it became the most serious wave of the pandemic. Every person that became sick was 33.23 percent less likely to vote, not including the 0.75 percent mortality rate. Combined, it cost Conservatives 92 thousand votes in PA, 36 thousand votes in AZ, 150 thousand votes in GA, and 61 thousand votes in WI. The Alpha-Alpha strain cost The President 380 thousand votes in FL, but Conservatives still held on there. To Jeffery's credit, he delivered his home state. He truly was a rising star. But the electoral college loss was too much to overcome.

The Former President took the loss with an unexpected quiet dignity. That was not in their calculations.

It had been over 100 years since an incumbent Liberal President had won reelection and had a unified House and Senate. More important than the loss was the statistical improbability of the outcome. Incumbent Presidents had a negative correlation with House and Senate votes. This was especially true for Liberal Presidents, unless they died in office, in which case the correlation flipped

95

positive. Since 1900, in cases where Liberal Presidents died in office, their Vice President won reelection and held a unified government 100 percent of the time. Billie and Wilma D. had not looked at this correlation before, because there were only two cases, and it did not come up as a statistically significant sample size.

Billie and Wilma D. initially believed that Jeffery Tripp Perez's stupidity was the exogenous factor that caused the statistically improbable outcome in the election. But that wasn't it—death was the factor they did not account for in their models. Death of the elected, or in this case, the electors, could be used to achieve statistically improbable outcomes in elections. This loss was devastating, but they would learn from it and update their numbers. They could then harness this tool to ensure future outcomes that would outperform any predictive model. They were now living life off the bell curve.

The President

The President sat in the Oval Office with the Davids. He had just given his victory speech. The results were declared the night before, but it was too late to do anything about it. He tried to stay up and watch, but as the hours wore on, he got too tired, and finally gave up at 9pm. He awoke in the morning to welcome news.

The Davids told him that not only had he won, but Liberals had also held on to control of the House and won the Senate.

The President thought to himself, *a majority in the House and Senate? That doesn't sound right. It was his second term. This didn't make sense.* "How did we win a majority in the House and Senate?" The President finally asked out loud.

The Davids seemed surprised that he had picked up on this. David W. tried to appeal to The President's ego to diffuse his concerns. "Yes sir, a great surprise. The country has spoken."

The President persisted, "No, it doesn't make sense. Something seems wrong. How did we sweep?"

David G. continued from where David W. left off, "Like I said Mr. President, you and @liceHerShe must have resonated with the voters."

Now, The President knew that was a lie. "Tell me. Did you have something to do with this Alpha-Alpha strain before the election?"

"Sir, what would you like me to say?" David W. asked, trying to keep a rueful grin from piercing the veil of contrition he was projecting.

The President was dumbfounded. He thought to himself, *hold on to this memory*. It was a struggle these days. He was tired ... What were they talking about? Then he said, "I wish I could remember."

He meant to say that in his head but said it out loud. He would have to run with it now.

David G. stepped forward. The Davids were huddled in a corner of the room to avoid sunlight, but this was important enough to draw David G. from the shadows. "Sir, I can help you with that if you'd like, but there would be no going back."

The President looked up at the Davids, "C'mon man. You don't think I know what you are? I know what you are. You haven't aged a day, and I have known you for 50 years. I'm no fool."

David W. was now out from lurking in the corner as well. As the Davids hovered over The President, David W. said, "Sir, I must warn you. If you go through with this, you will remember everything."

The President held steadfast. "I want to remember."

———

The President woke up in the middle of the night a few days later. He didn't remember going to bed. The last thing he remembered was talking to the Davids. He felt refreshed for the first time in years. He remembered. It was nice to have some clarity for once. He thought of how he had won his second term and swept the House and Senate. But then he remembered how he had won. The lives it had cost. The human suffering and the families that were broken up. He remembered all he had lost. He couldn't imagine inflicting that pain on someone else. It was unbearable.

It's odd. When you lose a child, the first thing people do is wonder if that was your only child. He knew they wondered that because that is what he used to think. It makes it seem as though they're a replaceable good. But the presence of another child doesn't make up for the loss of a child. He remembered what he had lost. He remembered going to the Davids and asking them to make him forget the pain he was in.

He didn't mean for this to happen on his watch. It was unfair. Other generations had not lived as long. His generation were pioneers in this regard. They were learning how to be old in the world with no template from previous generations. But like so many others of his generation, his ambition did not decline as he grew older. And when he finally got his opportunity, he was not in the correct mental state to make it work. It's unfair how 50 years of good service at lower positions could be undone by a few years of absent-mindedness when you reach your peak.

He left the bedroom of the presidential residence and told his Secret Service agents that he would like to go for a walk. As he walked, he watched the sunrise. He remembered other sunrises he had seen in his life and tried to compare them to this one, which he knew would be his last. As the sun rose, he faded away.

The Secret Service agents looked at each other, trying to figure out which of them would have to call this in.

@liceHerShe (She/Her)
(4.5 YEARS AFTER OPPOSITE DAY DECLARED)

@liceHerShe waited to be sworn in as the 47th President of the United States, and the first female to hold the office. This was a historic day. She was so humbled by this opportunity. She was in awe of her peers.

@liceHerShe was also sad that The President, who was now The Former President, had died. She was so blessed to have known him. He was an inspiration. She and the Davids looked desperately for someone to serve as Vice President. Unbelievably, they struggled to find anyone who wanted the position. Finally, they asked Chandra Brown, who accepted without hesitation.

They were lucky to have Chandra on the team. She had an amazing background. Her perseverance was truly an inspiration.

The Davids came in to see @liceHerShe and brought along Patricia Ocampo Santos. @liceHerShe was ecstatic to finally meet POS.

@liceHerShe shrieked, "OMG!!! POS!!! I'm such a big fan."

Patricia rolled her eyes, "POS is a name the people have bestowed on me. It is not for you to use. I am Patricia Ocampo Santos to you."

@liceHerShe was taken aback. She hadn't meant to be ignorant. She hoped this would start a conversation so she could better respect Patricia's truth. "I'm so sorry. Thank you for letting me know. I didn't mean to be ignorant. I hope this can start a conversation, and I can learn how to better respect your truth going forward."

Patricia also knew the importance of conversations. They were necessary to better understand the underrepresented. The only problem was that every time she started a conversation, others tried to talk. She was so sick of the represented and over-represented talking, and @liceHerShe was the embodiment of it all. How could she be The President? It was all a sick joke. "You're a disgrace. You shouldn't be here. It's a sick joke. Stay out of my way and we'll be fine. If you don't... well, let's just say that I know what you did in 2008."

@liceHerShe wondered how it would feel when she was outed. She knew it was just a matter of time.

She thought it would be terrible. She was wrong. She felt relieved, and excited in a way she hadn't felt in years.

No longer would she have to carry around the burden of her dark secret. She didn't realize how much this weight consumed her. It was as though her lungs had been working at half capacity these last few years and the bottleneck that was metering their use was suddenly cleared, bringing her lungs back to full capacity again and all at once.

She was so caught up in her relief, she barely noticed the Davids and Patricia leave the room. She stood in the middle of what now felt like an empty room. It would have been fully empty if not for the Secret Service agent who was assigned to remain with her.

@liceHerShe then realized she was not fully unburdened just yet. Patricia had only brought up the prospect of unburdening her from her dark secret. There was still the matter of telling the world. @liceHerShe thought, *if this is just the feeling of relief from the prospect of unburdening myself, imagine the relief I will feel when I actually tell the world.*

At that moment, telling the world her secret was the only feeling that existed to her. She felt like an addict, trying to recreate the high from her first time, but the mere prospect of telling the world would no longer achieve the same high. If she wanted to achieve that same feeling, she would have to escalate her behavior, and tell the world.

She cleared her throat as she prepared to say out loud what she had been holding back for so long. She then began doing what she previously considered unthinkable. She began saying out loud what she had kept bottled up for all these years.

"2007 was the beginning of the financial crisis, but professionally it was a good year for me. I made partner at my law firm. I was the youngest partner in the firm's history. That's the thing about corporate insurance law: good or bad economy, there are always insurance disputes.

"I was engaged to my partner, Max Triboro. He was sweet, kind, and gentle. He was everything a woman could want. You know, a neutered male, but not actually neutered. He wasn't an evil corporate lawyer like I was. He didn't care about money. He was a public defender. He wanted to follow in the footsteps of his grandfather, Thomas Triboro, and serve the public.

"Right off Harlem" @liceHerShe paused for a moment, "wait, can I say Harlem? I think so, but best to play it safe," she continued.

"In New York City between Manhattan, the Bronx, and Queens there is a bridge that connects those three boroughs: the Triboro Bridge, named of course after Thomas Triboro. Thomas Triboro was not a rich developer; he was a rich public servant. He served as the Parks Commissioner of New York for 30 years. From this position, he first built playgrounds, then he built parks, then he built bridges, then he built highways and public housing. He got things done, but he ruled with an iron fist."

"Excuse me… ma'am" the Secret Service agent spoke uncomfortably, trying to get @liceHerShe's attention.

But @liceHerShe was locked in and didn't notice the agent's overture. She continued,

"As I focused more on my career, my engagement to Max fell apart. But, we had so much mutual respect for each other; and so, we vowed to stay the closest of friends as we transitioned our relationship to focus on co-pet-parenting our two Pomeranians, Robby and Bobbi. Well, they were his Pomeranians because he had them before our relationship. But they became part of my life over the three months Max and I were together, and he assured me I would always be their step-pet parent.

"For a few weeks, I visited them on Saturday mornings; and for just those few hours, we were happy again. But then Max started dating. He asked me to stop coming by unannounced. He said I couldn't visit Robby and Bobbi anymore; it was getting awkward. But what kind of step-pet parent would I be if I didn't see them? He told me I wasn't really their step-pet parent, that he didn't even know what a step-pet parent was.

"I was lost, alone, and adrift. My friends were tired of watching me mope around, so they staged an intervention.

"They asked why I would even want to marry into that racist family anyway? *Racist family?* I had no idea what they were talking about. They told me Thomas Triboro was a well-known bigot. I thought there was no way that was true. Thomas Triboro was a public servant who built New York, and Max became a public defender to emulate him. Many of the people Max defended were Black, so how could the family be racist?

"That night, I looked on the internet and found nothing.

"Over the next few weeks, I couldn't shake the feeling that I was missing something. I threw myself into researching Thomas Triboro. At first, my research didn't yield much. But one day, while looking at a map I had created of all the parks and playgrounds Thomas Triboro built in the city, I noticed something.

"Of the 350 playgrounds that Thomas built in the city, 300 of them were in white upper-class neighborhoods, 48 of them were in white lower income and middle-class neighborhoods, one of them was in a Black middle-class neighborhood and one of them was in a Black lower-class neighborhood.

"That meant that 0.6 percent of the playgrounds built by Thomas Triboro were in Black neighborhoods, compared to the 12.0 percent of the NYC population that was Black during Thomas Triboro's tenure. Still, I didn't have the smoking gun. His focus on upper-class neighborhoods could have meant he was just a snob."

"Excuse me … ma'am," the Secret Service agent again sheepishly tried to break in, but to no avail.

@liceHerShe's eyes sank. She was coming to the painful part of her story. "A few weeks later, I was walking down the street in the middle of the day. I had quit my job to focus fully on my Thomas Triboro research, and I saw my step-pet children with their walker. I ran over to say hi to them, but both Robby and Bobbi barked at me like I was a stranger." @liceHerShe paused a moment to allow her audience to take in the palpable torment this part of the memory brought to her.

After her brief pause, @liceHerShe's eyes now narrowed, and her tone shifted, going from emotional trauma to fierce determination. "Max Triboro had chewed me up and spit me out like I was garbage. I couldn't let the Triboros get away with it. I called Max, but he said he didn't have time to talk. Max was now a prominent public defender, and claimed he was busy with a case. He was hailed by several civic associations for bringing high quality legal services to those who couldn't pay. But I saw through it. He was just like his grandfather. It wouldn't be long until he told his clients that they could no longer see their step pet-children.

"Thomas Triboro had been out of public office for 40 years and dead for 30 years at the time. The chance of finding someone who had worked with him seemed slim, but I didn't have to look too hard. They came out of the woodwork to speak with me. Members of his highway commission told me how he wanted to keep Black people out of his public works, so he limited public transportation to his parks and airports. He siphoned state and federal money away from hospitals and schools to build public highways for wealthier residents who owned cars. Members of his public housing commission spoke about how he hired corrupt developers who would not complete their work, in order to stifle the development of lower income housing.

"I went public with my findings. Many minority communities had been saying these things for years, but now I was talking about it. I took to social media, and the people responded. It was a long, hard battle, but we convinced the city to take the Triboro name off his precious flagship bridge."

@liceHerShe shook her head and looked down at the floor. "But my zeal for justice against the Triboro family came at a price. The best way to get my message out was through social media. I needed to increase my presence, and the best way to do this is to like other people's posts. So, that's what I did.

"My friend Julie went through a divorce around the same time my engagement fell apart. She was dating people and posted a picture with her new boyfriend. I wanted to support her, but more than that, I wanted to grow my presence. Without examining the picture, I liked it. Later that day, when I looked at the picture, I noticed that her boyfriend was wearing a sleeveless shirt. On his arm was a tribal tattoo. But he was of Irish decent, not tribal. In my eagerness to build a case against Thomas Triboro, I got sloppy. I was so focused on exposing this social injustice, I ended up blindly complying with cultural appropriation. I was no better than Thomas Triboro. I have been living with that guilt ever since.

"As it turns out, I never had to build my case against Max. After people found out what a racist his grandfather was, he could no longer get work as a public defender."

"Ma'am!" the Secret Service agent now said more forcefully. @liceHerShe looked up at the Secret Service agent. He now had her attention.

The Secret Service agent couldn't believe he had to do this, but there was no one else in the room. He had to say something. "Hi.

Sorry, Ma'am, I'm not supposed to do this, but to be honest, I am pretty freaked out because I just watched The Former President spontaneously turn to ash. I wasn't sure, but have you been talking to me?"

@liceHerShe looked around at the empty room, and then back at the agent, "Why, I guess so."

The Secret Service agent knew he was way out of line. "Madam President, I believe your party isn't coming back. It's my understanding you were supposed to be at your inauguration 20 minutes ago."

@liceHerShe looked around again at the empty room. She had been so wrapped up in her powerful story, that she hadn't yet noticed the obvious. "Oh … I guess I am all alone."

@liceHerShe realized the Davids were not coming back. She wasn't sure whom to consult. She felt overwhelmed.

The Secret Service agent saw @liceHerShe's bewildered look. He was terrified. How was she going to lead? Were they all doomed? If they were doomed, he might as well tell her. "That story about liking the picture was out weeks ago. It didn't have any impact on your approval rating. Well, in all fairness it would be hard to take your approval rating down further. I am only saying this because if and when someone takes a shot at you, I have to throw myself between you and the bullet. People are agitated about your presidency. There is nearly an open revolt in several states."

@liceHerShe was surprised, but she appreciated the agent speaking his truth. "Thank you for speaking your truth. What is your name?"

The Secret Service agent tried to regain his composure, "My name is Rex Keller," he then paused, but realizing he was addressing The President quickly added, "Ma'am," at the end of the sentence.

@liceHerShe felt a great comfort with the agent. He was the only one that stayed. Her loyal Rex Kellermam. "Well, Rex Kellermam, you're hired."

Rex was way off base. There was no way he was now going to correct her on his name. He was already severely in breach of his duty. He also had no idea what she was talking about. He was a Secret Service agent, what was she talking about, *he was hired?* The country was doomed, wasn't it? "Sorry, Ma'am, I'm not sure what you mean."

@liceHerShe laughed to herself. *That's such a classic Rex reaction. Oh, her dear loyal Rex Kellermam, when will he learn?* "Well, I am The President and I need advice. I don't see anyone else around or think anyone is coming. So, advise me. What do you think I should do?"

Before he could fully process the question, or if or how he should respond, Rex Kellermam snapped back, "Get your head out of your phone, stop posting, and act like a Goddamn President." As soon as he said it, he wanted to pull it back. What had he done? "I'm sorry, Madam President. I don't know why I said that. Please accept my apology."

Alice Hershe lifted her head out of her phone. For the first time in years, she wasn't thinking of her next post. She knew exactly what Rex meant. She needed to be more presidential.

Shawn Bennet

S hawn Bennet was a new type of congressman. He came to office on the Liberal wave that overtook the nation during the Alpha-Alpha outbreak. He was a Liberal from Tulsa, OK, one of the more Conservative districts in the country. The Alpha-Alpha strain had had a particularly devastating impact on Tulsa, because Tulsa was a district where Conservatives generally skipped the Spit Brothers Handshake in favor of spitting directly into each other's mouths.

In his last campaign for Mayor of Tulsa, Shawn had narrowed his loss to a mid-teens percentage. This was an improvement over the previous election when Shawn lost by 25 percent. Before getting into politics, Shawn was not used to losing.

Shawn was six-foot-five, handsome, and naturally liked people as much as they liked him. Shawn's father was Black, and his mother was a member of the Osage Nation, which made Shawn the only Black and Indian member of the Tulsa City Council.

Shawn knew there was hate in the world, but he had never personally experienced it. He was Black and he was Indian, and Tulsa had a bad history with both, but his good looks and affability had shielded him from the hatred others experienced. His paternal grandfather, James Bennet, had survived the Tulsa Race Massacre, while his maternal grandfather, Charles Roan, was the only member of his family not surreptitiously murdered for the oil rights belonging to Osage Indians.

But hearing stories of hate and experiencing it first-hand are two different things. Because Shawn was likeable, handsome, and smart, he always received the benefit of the doubt from others, which made Shawn a lifelong pragmatist. He assumed others would always act with best intentions, even if they had different views than him.

Shawn was one of the most well-liked members on the city council, but he was just too Liberal for the voters of the greater Tulsa area. Shawn was a Tulsa Liberal, which made him a Conservative in a lot of other parts of the country. That's why Shawn was surprised when the National Liberal Party asked him to run for Congress in his district. Shawn figured it was such an unwinnable race for any Liberal that the party wasn't thinking when they asked him.

But Shawn was happy to run. He didn't think he was going to win, but he had a reason for running. Shawn ran for Congress to bring attention to a personal cause: his grandmother had been scammed by a telemarketer. Shawn wanted Congress to do something to protect senior citizens from these scams, so he ran for office to bring attention to the subject. At best, he hoped his losing campaign would still draw enough publicity to shed light on the issue.

Unfortunately, due to the rules of Opposite Day, his campaign to end scams on senior citizens led the Conservative candidate to campaign for increased protections for scammers in the area. Why couldn't telemarketing and pyramid schemes become a booming industry for the greater Tulsa area? The region was rich in the natural resource of senior citizens; it was a shame not to take advantage of this abundance. The issue was adopted by the Oklahoma State Legislature, which prepared local tax incentives to attract scammers from as far away as Russia to set up call centers in Tulsa.

The call centers were a boon to the local economy. The incumbent Shawn was facing already had a massive lead heading into the election, and the economic windfall only widened it. Shawn didn't care about the electoral setback, but he was depressed that his attempt to protect seniors only put them in more danger. He was a political novice and couldn't believe that the rule of Opposite Day would so strictly apply to a race that was as big of a blowout as his was. In one instant, Opposite Day popped Shawn's lifelong bubble that others would act with the best of intentions. For the first time, Shawn saw that others would try to make him fail, not because it meant their success, but just for the pleasure of seeing him fail.

Then the Alpha-Alpha strain hit the city and claimed many lives. The next thing he knew, Shawn was the Congressman from Tulsa.

Along with Shawn, there were seven other Liberals from Conservative strongholds who won election due to the Alpha-Alpha wave. Their peers labeled them "The Walking Dead." They were not long for Washington, and there was no point investing time or resources into building relationships with any of them. They would be in office for one term. They were an anomaly. A temporary Liberal legislative convenience. To most other Liberals, they were non-adversarial warm bodies.

During mealtimes, The Walking Dead were ushered to a far-off table in the congressional cafeteria. It reminded Shawn of the table where the strange Conservative kids at his high school used to sit.

Before coming to Washington, Shawn had heard from friends that members of Congress were stupid. But he was skeptical of this claim. When Shawn got to Washington D.C., he realized how untrue it was.

If members of Congress were stupid, then how were they the greatest stock traders in the world? Shawn had previously thought that Wall Street was where the best stock traders in the world worked. But members of Congress were much better at trading stocks. They bought stocks right before the market went up and sold right before the market went down. Their timing was impeccable. They seemed to have a sixth sense for knowing when good or bad news would come out and impact the market.

The more Shawn learned about stock trading, the more confusing it became.

Frank Vultaggio was a fellow member of The Walking Dead. He was a Liberal from Staten Island, New York. Before Frank, every male member of Frank's family worked on the floor of the New York Stock Exchange. However, Frank saw that these jobs were being replaced by computers. He also wanted to learn how to trade stocks from the best, so he ran for Congress. The older generation in Frank's family was Conservative, but they said Frank was too young to join the Conservative Party. It was bad enough he was not entering the family business; they didn't want the neighbors to think he was some sort of young Conservative creep. So, Frank joined the Liberals.

Frank was a real-life, New York Italian. Shawn knew it was wrong, but he always wanted to meet a real New York Italian, like in the movies. It seemed so glamorous. He knew it was wrong to think of Frank as a stereotype, but living his life in Tulsa, Shawn hadn't come across many of these types, so it was a novelty for him. And Frank did not disappoint.

Before taking his seat at their table in the congressional cafeteria, Frank was on his cell phone. Shawn heard Frank say, "We want to buy SPUs for tomorrow" before he hung up the phone and sat down.

Shawn looked over as Frank took the seat next him. "Frank, how are you?"

"Can't complain, how you doin'?" Frank replied.

Shawn was ecstatic to hear him say it like that … *how you doin'?* It was so cool. Just like in the movies.

"I can't complain," Shawn replied. But Shawn was curious about what Frank had said on the phone. Shawn had been in Washington a few weeks and hadn't heard much about the impressive stock trades that Congress was so famous for. "Sorry to snoop, but I heard you on your phone. Were you doing something in the stock market? I don't know the first thing about it."

"Yeah … I'm sweatin' bullets over here. We got the jobs number coming out tomorrow. I'm buying the market into the number. I think it's gonna miss by a mile." Shawn wasn't 100 percent sure what Frank meant, but from context, he could tell it had something to do with the stock market.

Shawn knew that the 'jobs number' referred to the monthly employment numbers put out by the National Bureau of Labor Statistics on the first Friday of every month. The report showed how many jobs have been added or lost in the last month across the country. It was one of the most important real-time economic indicators.

From what Shawn could cobble together, he knew enough to ask, "Wait, why do you think it's going to miss by a mile?"

Frank wore an ear-to-ear grin. "A few weeks back, I met the head analyst who puts the report together." Frank made a poor attempt to cover up his sense of self-satisfaction, but the excitement in his voice was apparent. "I saw him on the street today. He looked completely out of sorts. Real nervous."

Shawn was starting to piece together what this meant from context. "And if you think the jobs number is going to miss, why are you buying the market? Isn't that bad for the economy?"

Frank chuckled, "Yeah, no shit it's bad for the economy. It's terrible for the economy. That's why you need to buy the market."

Shawn was back to square one again. "Sorry, I'm confused. If it's bad for the economy, then isn't that bad for the market?"

Frank impatiently shook his head, "Tulsa, what's wrong with you? It's not bad for the economy, it's terrible for the economy. That's good for the market." Frank now took on a tone that indicated what he was saying was self-evident. "The stock market doesn't want the economy to do well. All the companies that trade on the stock market need the economy to do well, but the overall market doesn't want that. The stock market only cares about what the Fed does with interest rates. If the economy is bad, then the Fed can't raise rates. If the economy is good, then they are more likely to raise rates."

Shawn was starting to understand again. He realized this was some Opposite Day nonsense. "Oh, so the stock market goes up when the economy does badly, and it goes down when the economy does well?"

"Ding ding ding… Tulsa, you may be good at something other than cow-fucking just yet," Frank replied.

Shawn thought to himself, *This guy is better than I could have imagined. If he bumps into someone and says, "I'm walkin' here," I may just lose it.* Shawn also wondered if anyone else was starting to get annoyed at this Opposite Day garbage.

The Davids (1/1)

(4.5 YEARS AFTER OPPOSITE DAY DECLARED)

The Davids sat with POS and Rory Cohen. They had just left a meeting with the largest Liberal Party donors after the inauguration.

The Davids were frustrated that Patricia let The President know that she knew her secret. There was no strategic advantage to letting The President know. It was another example of Patricia's emotions getting the best of her. But The Davids knew it was also her emotions that drove her meteoric rise.

"Patricia, don't you think you were particularly hard on The President?" David G. asked.

"I just can't help it," Patricia replied. "The fact that she is President is exactly what's wrong with the country."

Rory broke in, "You were completely out of control." He turned to the Davids, "David, do you see what I have to deal with here? It's completely unreasonable."

Patricia rolled her eyes, "Whatever, Shylock. Don't you have some rent to collect or a family to evict?"

Patricia and Rory were not getting along like the Davids had hoped they would. They were both so stubborn. If they could stop bickering, they would realize that their true potential was together. Only together could they achieve what they needed to.

The Davids were growing tired of the bickering, tired of Patricia's petulance, and tired of Rory's inability to control Patricia. David W.

interjected, "That's enough! Both of you! Don't snatch defeat from the jaws of victory. Everything is working perfectly. If you two could just get along, you would see that everything is coming together."

Patricia was unconcerned about David W.'s wrath. "I don't see why I had to go to that meeting. It was just stuffy, rich elites. I represent the people. Those were not the people. Each one of them was either a womanizer, or a tax cheat, or a closet Conservative…"

David G. stopped Patricia mid-sentence. "That's enough. What those people have in common with each other, and even with you, is that they are focused on their impact on the world on a larger scale, but in order to enact the changes they seek, they must work extra hard."

David W. continued, "If they held themselves to the standards they set, they would become bogged down in regulation. Once they have fully achieved their goals, then of course they will have the luxury of holding themselves to those standards."

"Of course. I totally get that," Patricia replied. "But it just seems very off-brand for me to be with people like them."

David G. tried to assure her, "It's not off-brand. You're sending the message to the people that you are willing to do anything to get done what needs to be done."

David W. looked deep into Patricia's eyes and chanted, "There is no one else who can do it."

Before David W. could repeat his chant, Rory snorted. "Yeah, even if that means taking up Olivia Von Vondenbergen on her invitation."

After hearing Rory interject, Patricia snapped out of the lull the Davids were talking her into. "No chance!" she shot back.

The Davids couldn't believe how tactless Rory was. During the reception with Liberal Donors, Olivia Von Vondenbergen invited Patricia to the Natural History Museum Gala. Every year on the first Tuesday in March, Olivia Von Vondenbergen hosted the Natural History Museum Gala. It was sort of a charity event. Not the kind of charity that fed anyone, cured anything, or put anyone through school, but it did stop traffic. All the A-listers would be there. The Davids knew this was the type of event they needed Patricia to go to, and at worst, it would be a great bonding experience for her and Rory … if they didn't kill each other by then.

The Davids grew tired of playing to Patricia's ego And Rory's incessant bickering. David G. looked at Rory and Patricia and said, "You're both going."

Rory and Patricia could tell from David's use of the word *both* that he meant business.

Ted Cruise

onda Civic, Honda CR-V, Honda Fit, Honda NSX, Honda Prelude, Honda S600, Honda S500, Honda S800, Honda S2000, Hyundai Elantra, Hyundai Accent, Hyundai Sonata, Jaguar XK120, Jaguar C-Type ....

5.0 YEARS AFTER OPPOSITE DAY DECLARED

Patricia Ocampo Santos (Me/Me)
(5.0 YEARS AFTER OPPOSITE DAY DECLARED)

It was the second Tuesday in March. All preparations were made for the Natural History Museum Gala. Hungry orphans showed up at the steps of the museum after hearing there was a charity event and thinking they could get a hot meal. They were shooed away and told it wasn't that kind of charity. The A-Listers were about to arrive.

Each year, Olivia Von Vondenbergen chose a unique theme for the gala. This year's theme was the Roman emperor Caligula. When Patricia found out the theme, she became even more resistant to the idea of going. The Roman Empire was the predecessor of modern-day colonialism. How could she go to a gala that celebrated its history? The Davids were insistent that she go, but said if she wanted, she could use it as a forum to stick it to the elites.

Before Patricia could commit to attending, she made sure the gala conformed to her dietary restrictions. Patricia enforced a strict dietary code on herself and her staff. Neither she, nor any of her staff, were allowed to eat or be in the same room as cuisine of one culture that was prepared by a chef from a different culture. There were some exceptions. Pizza, for instance, could be made by anyone. Fusion cuisine was particularly dicey but was OK if the chef was from the more subjugated culture of the combination.

The gala was supposed to be the big break for Ana Menano, a young Portuguese chef. She prepared authentic cuisines from each part of the Roman Empire that would be passed around as hors d'oeuvres. A nervous staffer for Olivia Von Vondenbergen replaced Ana, thinking that her Portuguese background would not be considered diverse enough to serve these cuisines. However, at the last minute, Patricia's staffers communicated that Ana did qualify to serve cuisines from across most of the Roman Empire, except for the Middle Eastern and Northern African portions. Ana was rehired, and the dishes from the Middle East and North Africa were scrapped. Olivia Von Vondenbergen was concerned that throwing away the Middle Eastern and North African dishes would attract more hungry orphans to the gala, so she instructed her staff to take food and put it in a dumpster five miles away from the museum. The orphans were not savvy and had no idea the tightly wrapped bundles that were taken from the museum by staffers were the hot meals they were looking for. The hungry orphans left before the A-listers arrived.

Patricia stepped onto the red carpet of the Natural History Museum Gala. Rory stood next to her. The Davids insisted she make Rory her plus-one for the event. She wore an off-the-shoulder white satin dress. Reporters flocked to her. One thing that was apparent, but no one ever dared mention out loud: she was beautiful, and she looked gorgeous in the dress. As she twirled for the cameras, it became clear that the dress had a message written on the back. Reporters salivated. They begged her to stop twirling so they could get a better look at the message. There on the back of POS's dress in bold letters was the message, "Increase Taxes on Some of the Wealthy by Changing the Time Period for the Carried Interest Provision of Capital Gains Carry-Forward from 3 to 5 Years."

The reporters ate it up. They immediately nicknamed the garment the "Increase Taxes on Some of the Wealthy by Changing the Time Period for the Carried Interest Provision of Capital Gains Carry-Forward from 3 to 5 Years" dress. Patricia was the star of the red carpet. She went inside; the place looked extravagant. It was the grandest ballroom she had ever seen, and she felt like a princess. She thought to herself that Olivia Von Vondenbergen had impeccable taste. Patricia looked around the room and realized she could get some ideas for her next Taco Tuesday from here.

While Patricia was a hit with the press outside, her reception from other guests at the gala was icy at first. Slowly, guests checked their phones, and eventually came up to Patricia to congratulate her on her bold statement. First, she was approached by the actors and athletes in attendance. Then the influencers and fashionistas. Finally, Patricia was approached by the only businesspeople at the gala, a small subsect of Liberal private equity executives Olivia Von Vondenbergen found tasteful enough to include.

Patricia remarked to Rory how strange it was that everyone was so cold at first. Rory explained that they were checking the tax implications of her dress with their accountants. Each group only came over after they confirmed that her proposal would have little to no financial impact on them. Patricia was impressed—for everything that she hated about Rory, he was somewhat useful to have around.

The gala was spectacular and Patricia, her dress, and even Rory were the brightest attractions. Olivia Von Vondenbergen had outdone herself. Ana Menano's cuisine was exquisite. Servers dressed as authentic Romans brought around hors d'oeuvres. Every 45-minute interval featured a new cuisine from a different civilization conquered by Rome. Each was better than the next, and Patricia thought to herself that she would have liked to see what Ana had put together for the Middle East and North Africa, but quickly banished the thought to the back of her mind. The food was delicious. The room was filled with people who didn't eat much, but all were taking the hors d'oeuvres by the fistful.

After the third round of hors d'oeuvres, servers brought around buckets. Guests began vomiting in the buckets as the servers continued holding them. Patricia looked to Rory when a server presented him with a bucket. He reminded her that the theme of the party was Caligula. Also, their culinary tour of The Roman Empire still had France and Greece. He then said, "When in Rome," and vomited in the bucket held by the server.

Patricia held off on vomiting. As the night continued, she ate more and more and talked to more and more people. She made sure to stay on message with everyone. Olivia Von Vondenbergen came over just as the servers completed the French portion of the hors d'oeuvres. Patricia was always embarrassed by it, but she loved French food. She told friends that she was being ironic in her love for French food, but her friends knew that she was humorless and incapable of irony.

As Olivia Von Vondenbergen walked over, Patricia noticed that she looked less harsh than she did last time. If she had to think of an adjective to describe it, she would say Olivia looked peaceful.

Olivia Von Vondenbergen approached Patricia and Rory, stopped a few feet in front of them, kissed in the air, turned her head, and kissed in the air again. Then she clasped her hand to her chest as she greeted them. "Darling, I'm so glad you could make it. I must say, you look fabulous in the dress. But it's not just the dress, it's everything. I love it all. Brava."

"Thank you for having us. This is really a unique gala you put together." Patricia knew she had to be on her best behavior, but she was also genuinely having a great time. "It's a lot of fun. The food is amazing. I'm so happy it's for a good cause."

Patricia realized she wasn't exactly sure what the charity being supported by the gala was. She looked around the room and thought with all these wealthy people here, they must have raised a lot of money. "Are you happy with the amount you raised? Also, sorry, I forgot, what exactly is the cause we're supporting?"

Patricia was starting to feel sick. She had overdone it on the French food.

Olivia Von Vondenbergen sighed in a friendly manner. "Oh, you darling girl. This isn't that type of charity. You have so much to learn. Rory, what are you teaching her?"

Rory looked bashful when he answered, "I'm teaching her as much as she is teaching me. She is a true believer."

Patricia was taken aback. *Was that an actual compliment from Rory?*

Patricia tried to hide her surprise and keep the small talk going with Olivia. This is what the Davids and Rory called *playing the game, and* Patricia had promised the Davids and Rory that she would try to *play the game* at the gala.

Patricia saw Olivia as a Liberal in name only. Olivia was well-intentioned enough to be Liberal, but she was not fully committed. Normally Patricia would demolish her. She would find something Olivia had said or done in the past and demand an apology. Once Olivia apologized, it would be over. Everything Olivia said or did from there would be tainted, her influence would be lost, and the name Olivia Von Vondenbergen would ring through the generations as a cautionary tale to other Liberals that were not fully committed.

Instead, Patricia kept her promise to remain on her best behavior and asked, "What has been your favorite course so far? I'm not sure how you can be around all this delicious food."

Olivia Von Vondenbergen laughed haughtily. "Oh dear, I don't eat. I am on a liquid diet. It's part of my new skin treatment."

"I was going to say, you look great. What are you doing?" Patricia asked.

"I am trying a new treatment with my dermatologist. He has been injecting small amounts of embalming fluid into my face. It makes me look less harsh. It's the latest thing. I would say you should try it, but you already have perfect skin." Olivia Von Vondenbergen felt comfortable telling others about her new skin treatment because it had been done on a routine trip to her dermatologist. It wasn't anything as vulgar as plastic surgery.

"Well, I would say you looked exquisite before, and you look exquisite now," Rory interjected with an uncharacteristically tactful response.

Patricia couldn't believe that Rory was able to say something charming. However, her surprise was soon overshadowed by a rumbling sensation in her gut. Patricia recognized that she was starting to feel sick. She was glad Rory was there to help her through the conversation with Olivia. He was very intuitive and could tell she wasn't feeling well. Patricia began to sweat, as holding down the French food became her main priority.

Olivia Von Vondenbergen got back to focusing on the dress. "But my dear, you simply must tell me about this dress."

Patricia powered through her queasiness. This was no time to get sick. This had the potential to be a teachable moment. She could show Olivia the error of her ways, and Olivia would see it because she was well intentioned. And then Olivia could use her influence and tell her powerful friends. And then Olivia and her powerful friends would all say to themselves, *You know what, Patricia is completely right and I am completely wrong.* Then they would finally be the right kind of Liberals, and they would credit Patricia for their political epiphany. And then Patricia would be voted "Greatest Politician of the Year", the award that had always eluded her. "Well, it's more about the message," Patricia explained. "There is a growing disparity in this country between the haves and the have-nots. The only ones who can fix this is the government. We must take power away from the powerful and give it to ourselves, so we can better help the powerless."

One of the servers came over with a bucket. Teachable moment or not, Patricia was having trouble keeping the food down. But she persisted, "If we want to close the income gap, the government needs to be larger to ensure equitable distribution among citizens."

Blahhhhhhh. Patricia began throwing up the hors d'oeuvres into the bucket.

When she was done, she looked up at Olivia. She saw her teachable moment slipping away. "I'm so sorry about that," she said, feeling bashful for the first time in years.

To Patricia's surprise, Olivia Von Vondenbergen seemed unfazed. "Oh, don't think twice about it." Patricia could tell that Olivia meant to say this in a way that was assuring.

Patricia then looked at the server who stood there stoically. She realized she got some vomit on him. "Sorry about that. I got a little on you," she said to the server.

"Don't talk to the help!" Olivia snapped as she uncharacteristically lost her cool.

Patricia didn't realize how seriously Olivia took the theme of the party. "Oh, because of the theme of the party?"

"Sure. Yes," Olivia said as she tried to regain her composure.

As the server turned around to walk away, Rory stopped him. "Hey, would you mind hanging by here another moment? Just in case." Patricia was glad Rory asked the server to stick around.

Patricia tried to salvage her teachable moment, "So where was I? The government needs to be bigger so it can take a more active role in people's lives." But as much as Patricia persisted, so did the French Food. "The more active the government can become, the happier everyone will be. It is the only way to solve the income disparity between the rich and poor."

Blahhhhhhhhh! Patricia was throwing up the French round of the hors d'oeuvres. But this wasn't like the vomiting of the other guests, who vomited to clear room in their stomachs for the next course. The mixture of foie gras and escargot was too rich for Patricia, and she was projectile vomiting into the bucket.

Olivia was taken aback at this most distasteful display. It was one thing to elegantly vomit and clear room for more hors d'oeuvres. But to heedlessly throw up out of necessity like a sick child was unforgivable. This had the unthinkable potential of becoming *a scene.*

"Oh my. I'll give you a moment." Olivia excused herself from the conversation.

Rory stood by Patricia's side while she finished vomiting. Patricia felt better after she finished, but it was probably best that she not face the press outside. Rory escorted her to a private exit through the garage. They walked two avenues over to avoid being spotted and hailed a cab.

Residents of Patricia's district had found out that she was in NYC, so she felt like she had to stay in her district for the night. Rory stayed with her in the cab.

Rory Cohen (It/It) and
Patricia Ocampo Santos (Me/Me)
(5.0 Years after Opposite Day Declared)

Rory and Patricia rode up the West Side Highway in the cab. They were on their way to Patricia's district. She didn't have security with her, and Rory wanted to make sure that no one in her district bothered her with complaints. She was elected to represent a social agenda, not deal with the day-to-day whims of a few constituents. Most constituents saw the bigger picture, but there was always the riffraff.

Patricia couldn't believe what she was about to say, but she had to say it. "Rory, thanks for helping me get out of there."

"Of course. It's what I'm here for," Rory said in a nonchalant manner that felt alien to him. "You were great tonight, by the way. Your message really resonated with people after they realized they'd be exempt from your tax demands."

Patricia shook her head, "I'm very embarrassed."

"Why? Don't be. That was the point of the gala," Rory said in a comforting tone. Rory felt awkward as he said it. What was he doing? Patricia was vulnerable. That never happened. He needed to go in for the kill and get the upper hand. Didn't he need to let her know that he had this over her? If he comforted her, she wouldn't respect him. She would have the upper hand.

Patricia took comfort in Rory's consolation. "I can imagine Olivia Von Vondenbergen's face when she saw how much I threw up."

Rory laughed, "Don't worry about her. Her monocle almost fell out, though."

Patricia looked up with a confused expression. "Wait. She wears a monocle?"

"No, that's a joke. Sorry," Rory explained. "She just seems like one of those really uptight older white women."

Patricia understood jokes, but they normally just made her angry. This one seemed funny. She wasn't sure what to do after a funny joke. Was she supposed to laugh? How do you even laugh? When was the last time she laughed? Wouldn't that be a weird thing to do?

Before Patricia could figure out how to react, the cab stopped. They were at her apartment. Rory came upstairs with her. They sat in her kitchen and talked as the seconds of small talk blended into minutes of conversation, which melted into hours of discussion.

"Did you mean what you said tonight?" Patricia asked. "When you said you were learning about being a true believer?"

Rory felt so stupid for saying that. Now she had the upper hand. But she didn't seem like she was on the attack. Maybe he should just answer the question. "Yeah … I know it's been bumpy at times with us, but this is a really interesting experience. There's a lot we can accomplish together. I've worked with a lot of politicians but have never seen this kind of opportunity before."

Patricia couldn't believe what she was hearing. Rory was finally admitting that she was right. He was such a fool for opening up. Now she had the upper hand. But the upper hand felt different this time. Maybe that wasn't her goal in this conversation. Maybe Rory was trying to connect with her. "Why is that? Why have you always worked with politicians? Why not run yourself?" she asked.

Rory looked sheepish, "Me? Run? Nah. It would be impossible. I have too many skeletons in the closet." What was he doing? Why would he open that door? Although Rory had to admit, it felt good, even exciting to let someone in.

"Oh, because of all the killers you helped set free?" Patricia asked.

"No. You kidding me?" Rory replied. "I was keeping people out of jail. As long as you're not putting people in jail you can get votes."

"So, what is it? What're these dark secrets from your past?" Patricia was intrigued. She couldn't help herself.

"It's not from my past. It's nothing," Rory felt a sense of desperation. He had gone too far. Was it still possible to walk it back?

"C'mon." Patricia wondered why she was prying like this. Was she really interested? Yesterday she couldn't imagine anything worse than being caught in an elevator with Rory. Now she was asking him about dark secrets from his past. Why did she care? Was it the magic of the night? She had a feeling that whatever Rory was hiding was important for her to know.

She persisted, "Just tell me. Don't be such a baby." She paused as she realized what she said, adding, "Not to disparage babies, who are an important and underrepresented group in society, of course."

Patricia hated herself for saying that. She knew better. Real change couldn't happen unless we scrubbed our everyday language of pejorative colloquial phrases.

Rory had never let anyone get this far. Why was he confiding in her? It was as though he had no defenses, and his common sense was overtaken by an instinct desperate to connect with another person. "It's nothing. It's just … ah fuck it."

Rory took a deep breath before continuing. "The Davids already know, and chances are he would tell you one day anyway … I have an odd sexual thing. I can't get off unless someone steps on my balls and calls me a dirty Jew. I've been alone for years because of it." The words rushed out of Rory's mouth. Now that he had started, he couldn't stop, no matter how much he wanted to. "A few years ago, I started a website to find others with the same desires as me. Out of the entire internet, I could only find one other person who was interested, and she was too afraid to meet up. Do you know how much weird stuff there is on the internet? Only *one person*."

Patricia sat there with her mouth wide open. She couldn't believe it. "Oh my ..."

She tilted her head and looked at him.

Rory Interrupted her. "Don't look at me like that! I don't need your judgement."

Patricia tilted her head the other way. She was speechless.

"Well ... say something ..." Rory pleaded. "I should go ... this was a mistake ... you forced me to say it ... if you think about using this against me, I'll bury you." Rory looked at the window. They were on the fifth floor, so if he jumped, that would be it. He would not be around for Patricia to use this against him.

Patricia still couldn't find the words. She squinted. Finally, she was able to respond with a single word, "Dreyfusdidit?"

Rory was stunned. If she claimed not to know about his predilections, then how did she know his username for his website? Was this a setup? He wouldn't go down without a fight. He would take her and the Davids with him.

He looked at Patricia, who was gazing at him. He was surprised by her countenance. She didn't have the look she normally did when she went in for the kill. Did he misinterpret? Did she phrase that as a question? That would be impossible. Could she be? "QweensIsabella89?" Rory said half responding and half asking.

Patricia froze. She knew this couldn't be a coincidence. She knew the Davids engineered this. But she didn't care. Why Rory? Why did it have to be Rory? He had grown on her over the last few months, and their initial feelings of antipathy gradually turned to a mutual dependence, which both masked with a façade of acrimony that was starting to feel forced. He kept her on her toes, and she needed that. But a white male? It was so cliché.

For the first time in his life, Rory felt like he wasn't alone. He had searched the world for a companion and couldn't find one. When he could not find a companion, he increased the parameters of his search to not only include space, but time as well. Still, he could not find one. Now after searching through space and time, a companion sat in front of him. Now that he wasn't alone, he could stop looking to the past, in search of a period in which he fit in. He could now look to the future, to where they would build their lives.

————————

Rory and Patricia stared into each other's eyes. They saw a future together, one that went past the next few days. Past the next election. Past a time when the majority imposed their will on the oppressed. Past a time when the oppressed called on the government to get bigger and even the playing field. Past a time when even the oppressed realized that once a government gets bigger it cannot shrink. It can accelerate or decelerate its growth, but it cannot shrink, because a government that shrank was a dying government. Past a time when even the once-oppressed lost their senses and tried to deter the government from the task they had set in motion. Past the time when elections were paused so the people could regain their senses. This was the renegade government that brought them out of oppression after all; they fought the establishment, it's not like the government was now the establishment. They saw a future of perfect equality.

Patricia and Rory continued their work in government. Patricia was in a leadership position, but she was not the leader. She was a prominent member of the Standing Committee of the Politburo, the leaders' inner circle that helped run the government. Rory went back to practicing law. But instead of helping murderers stay out of prison, he worked at the Department of Justice, keeping people in prison.

But not murderers, just those out to murder the society that he and Patricia helped build.

Class was no longer based on money. Class structure would have been abolished altogether, but someone needed to be in charge. Therefore, the ruling class ruled, not to enrich themselves, but out of a noblesse oblige. The ruling class received some special privileges, but it was nowhere near the inequity that had prevailed before. Whereas before, when a few had so much and others had so little, now everyone had some, but not too much. Everyone could continue to have some if the crops didn't fail. The harvests held steady.

The ruling class kept their promise on inequality by not taking too much for themselves. But then the ruling class had children. Even those with the discipline to hold themselves to equal standards with their subjects still want what's best for their children.

The children of the ruling class were known as the princelings. The ruling class determined that the princelings would be the ruling class of the future. To ensure the princelings were ready to govern the people, the princelings needed special training. This was not a privilege; it was an obligation to the people. The princelings were put through rigorous training. They needed special schools, so the people built special schools. Many of the princelings were sent away to study at the finest schools abroad so they could bring home what they had learned. Because of their rigorous training, the princelings needed more resources and better food than the people. The princelings worked hard, and deserved some leisure, so they were given resources for leisure. Still, this was not the inequality that had prevailed before.

But a growing number of dissatisfied people complained. They said the princelings were too detached from the people. There was even some dissension within the ruling class, from members who had been there since the beginning. Rory helped take care of them, but stories of their demise made it to the people. The dissenters became martyrs. Then the people began to dissent. So, the leader brought back elections to allow the people to decide as they had in the past. The leader and the ruling class won their election, receiving 110 percent of the vote. Still, the people were dissatisfied. Whereas before, everyone had some; now a few had an increasing amount and the people had less, but still some. Still, everyone could have some if the crops didn't fail.

The crops failed.

———————

Patricia and Rory looked at each other. They were back in Patricia's kitchen on the night of the Natural History Museum Gala. They knew exactly what had gone wrong in their society and how to fix it. To build their society of equality, they needed a stronger foundation. They could not build a society with dissenters among them. They would need to purge the dissenters that had been with them from the beginning right away. There was only room for true believers.

That was tomorrow's work. Patricia kicked off her shoes and began to stretch out her feet. By the time she was done with Rory, he would have a permanent limp.

Ted Cruise

Pontiac Astre, Pontiac Aztek, Pontiac Bonneville, Pontiac Firebird, Pontiac Grand Am, Porsche 356, Porsche 550, Porsche 911, Porsche 904, Porsche 906, Porsche 908, Porsche 914, Porsche 917 ....

Shawn Bennet

As a member of The Walking Dead, Shawn couldn't get any momentum on his proposed legislation to protect senior citizens from fraud. Every day, he approached fellow Liberal members of Congress, but they ignored him. Since he would be gone in 18 months, he was of no use to them. When he did get a response, he was told most senior citizens were Conservatives, so let the Conservatives protect them. Every day, he and the other members of The Walking Dead were ushered off to the boondocks of the congressional cafeteria to sit by themselves.

Some of The Walking Dead had success branching out. Frank Vultaggio had some success thanks to his strategy of following around the lead analyst from The National Bureau of Labor Statistics. Frank studied the analyst's routine; from what time he left his house in the morning to what time he showed up at the office. The analyst was easy to read— all Frank needed to do was see him on the street before the jobs number came out and he could easily tell what the number would be. If the analyst looked nervous or worried, that meant the number was bad, and Frank would buy the market before the data. If the analyst looked calm or relaxed, that meant the number was good, and Frank would sell the market before the data. Before long, Frank amassed a large following.

Every month before the jobs number was announced, Frank was invited to sit with an influential group of congressional leaders. He would tell them what the jobs number would be like the next day. Those members then traded the market based on that information. The strategy worked. Frank figured out a way to get an edge on the jobs data. Frank, the Congressional leaders, and anyone Frank told about the data did very well.

As Frank's strategy continued to work, his following grew larger. It expanded from Liberal members of the House to Liberal members of the House and Senate. Soon, it even included some Conservative members of Congress. Even though the rules of Opposite Day were still in effect, members of Congress came together on a few occasions to consult with members from the opposite party. The most celebrated case of this was after the invention of the vaccine during the pandemic.

The country applauded as members of Congress set aside their differences and devised a cohesive plan for how to distribute the vaccine. Since first responders were so brave during the height of the pandemic and continued to be in danger from exposure, Congress determined that they should be at the front of the line. Because the elderly were the most vulnerable to the effects of the pandemic, Congress determined the elderly should also be at the front of the line. So, Congress came together, and without partisan fighting, determined that first responders and the elderly should be given the vaccine right after members of Congress received their doses. Members of both parties agreed that there was too much skepticism among the population about the long-term effects of the vaccine; so, to quell the public's concerns about the long-term effects, Congress would take the vaccine first, to show the people that there were no short-term effects to be concerned about.

Shawn needed to find a way to break free from his confinement to The Walking Dead. His salvation came with an invitation to join the Liberal wing of the Native American Caucus. Originally, the Caucus was made up of six congressional members from the House and Senate, two Liberal and four Conservative. After Opposite Day, the Liberal and Conservative members could no longer caucus together, so they split into two groups. However, when The Former President won his election, he brought one of the Liberal members of the Native American Caucus into his cabinet. As a result, there was only one member of the Liberal Native American Caucus before Shawn Bennet was elected.

Becky Werner was a Senator representing Massachusetts, and like Shawn, she was originally from Oklahoma. She was one of the whitest people in the world. Before Shawn was elected, she was the last Liberal member of the Native American Caucus, or as she insisted on saying, she, "was the last of the Mohicans."

Becky claimed Indian heritage early in her career, which made everyone feel uncomfortable. Before the declaration of Opposite Day, it was rumored she was going to come clean. However, after Opposite Day was declared, Conservatives picked up on this weakness and ridiculed her. Becky Werner had no choice but to lean in hard to her "identity".

She changed the way she dressed. She changed the way she talked. Conservatives knew she did not want to draw attention to this aspect of her work in the Senate. When Shawn Bennet was elected, Conservatives questioned why she did not restart the Liberal Wing of the Native American Caucus. Becky Werner had no choice but to lean into the role harder and invite Shawn to help start the Liberal Wing of the Native American Caucus.

When Shawn received the invitation to join her for lunch, he was torn. He was desperate to get out of his isolation, and he was proud of his heritage, but he didn't like how Becky Werner portrayed herself and he didn't like how she portrayed his heritage.

However, the news from home about senior citizens was getting worse. More call centers were popping up and reports of senior citizens being scammed out of their savings were becoming more common. Shawn had to do something to protect them. He let this objective override his distaste for Becky and accepted her invitation. They would meet for lunch in the congressional cafeteria on Tuesday … a Taco Tuesday.

The Committee to Unify National Tories

(5.0 YEARS AFTER OPPOSITE DAY DECLARED)

Like a well-groomed but very dumb phoenix, Jeffery Tripp Perez rose from the ashes of the Conservative electoral defeat. He was the future of the party.

The more research Billie and Wilma D. did, the more they found that death was the variable that could guarantee unprecedented electoral success. The Alpha-Alpha strain had shown them the value that death of the electorate could play. Now, the question was how to harness it.

Billie and Wilma D. knew that if they were looking for death, they needed an extremely volatile issue. Something that stoked the passions not only of those impacted, or those indirectly impacted, but of those not involved at all. They both knew which subject best fulfilled these criteria. It had to be the Middle East.

Billie and Wilma D. would have loved to avoid this topic. The Middle East was one of two positions in the Conservative platform they could not reconcile. Billie and Wilma D. could not understand how Conservatives favored Israel over its neighbors. Conservatives resisted change from Liberals. Similarly, many of Israel's neighbors resisted change of any sort for centuries. There was a clear code of conduct. The government declared what you could do, and especially what you could *not* do. If you broke the law, there were consequences. Billie and Wilma D. couldn't understand how Conservatives wouldn't favor this system.

Similarly, Billie and Wilma D. could not understand how Liberals disliked Israel. In a sea of law and order, Israel was a bastion for many of the Liberal ills that plagued domestic policy. There was a plurality of cultures and orientations; the people talked back to the government and hid behind their precious civil rights. It was chaos. It was exactly the kind of society that Liberals preferred. Liberals hated them.

This phenomenon was not the result of Opposite Day. The rules of Opposite Day did not apply to this part of the world. The Middle East wasn't locked in a conflict of Opposite Day, they were engaged in the "He Started It" wars. During conflicts in the region, combatants fought and did their respective damage. Afterwards, their supporters pointed their fingers at the opponent and proclaimed, "He Started It!"

Conservatives thought Israel's neighbors started it. Liberals thought Israel started it. Billie and Wilma D. believed there was a variable they were not grasping. They sensed that Liberals who vehemently thought Israel started it and Conservatives who were convinced Israel's neighbors started it used this conflict as a proxy to express a deep-seated opinion about something in the conflict other than who started it. But Billie and Wilma D. could not quite determine what that was.

Normally, Billie and Wilma D. could count on The Former Former President to stoke conflict about the region. The Former Former President was masterful at this. He clearly thought Israel's neighbors started it. The more he said it, the more Liberals insisted that Israel started it. By the end of his term in office, The Former Former President did so much for Israel that it became one of the main targets for Liberals looking to undo his legacy. But Billie and Wilma D. didn't want to rely on The Former Former President, they wanted to try out their rising star.

Shawn Bennet and Becky Werner (She/Her)

(5.0 YEARS AFTER OPPOSITE DAY DECLARED)

When Shawn walked into the cafeteria for his meeting with Becky Werner he was taken aback. POS had returned from her trip to the Natural History Museum Gala with a lot of ideas for Taco Tuesday. She really outdid herself. The cafeteria was transformed overnight. Mariachi and Banda performers were flown in, staff members of the cafeteria were dressed to celebrate different festivities from Dia de Muertos to the Guelaguetza Festival. For the meal, chefs from the hottest restaurants in Mexico City were flown in.

To quell pushback from farm state members on the increasing cost of Taco Tuesdays, the chefs were instructed to curate this week's menu around dishes made from domestically grown corn. The deal to use domestically grown corn for Taco Tuesday was brokered by Molly Cutler, a member of The Walking Dead from Iowa. POS wasn't sure about the appropriation implications of using corn from the US for Mexican dishes, so she boycotted the lunch just to be safe.

In the center of it all was a miniature replica of the Castillo de Kukulkan Pyramid, which was made small enough to fit inside the cafeteria, though Shawn was pretty sure a structural load-bearing wall had to be altered for it. It all looked impressive, but Shawn wondered how much this must have cost.

Shawn found his way to the table where Senator Becky Werner waited for him. He liked most of the other members of The Walking

Dead but was thankful for the change of scenery. If nothing else, Becky had been around for a while, so she could point him in the right direction of how to get momentum on his proposed legislation.

As they sat and talked, Shawn was surprised. He found Becky personable. Despite his misgivings before the lunch, he started to like her. She was even funny at times. But then the comments started.

As they ate their meal, Becky remarked, "This is amazing. I never knew so many dishes could be made from corn. You know, corn, or 'maize' as our ancestors called it, was a staple of the Native American diet."

Shawn brushed off the comment. He wanted to find out how to gain momentum on his bill. If he only had 18 months, he would at least make sure he followed through on his promise.

"Becky, I was wondering... I reached out to your office about a bill to protect senior citizens from fraud," Shawn explained. "It's a passion for me. I'm having trouble getting traction."

Becky said with a stoic look on her face, "Yes, I read your ideas. They are noble, just like our heritage. I respect what you are trying to do, but it involves telecoms legislation, so it will get to get bogged down. Think decades."

Shawn felt a sense of desperation. He had come to Congress by such a slim chance, it couldn't be for nothing. "But these people are stealing from the elderly. There must be something we can do."

Sensing Shawn's determination, Becky said, "Well, if you are really committed to this, you need to be on the right committees. This would fall under Energy and Commerce. Are you on that committee?"

Shawn felt deflated, "No. I am on the House Administration Committee."

"Well, before you can even think about getting this done, you need to become a member. No one will be receptive to anything you have to say on the issue until you are on that committee. How would you feel if you were on a committee, and someone with no history on the committee just came in and started acting as if they were a member all along? Wouldn't it annoy you to see them falsely lay claim to your committee's identity?" Becky asked without a hint of irony in her voice.

Shawn held his tongue. After all, Becky was giving him the most helpful advice he had received since he arrived in Washington. "Becoming a member of that committee is going to be a challenge. I'm only going to be here for one term. I won't have the chance to get another committee assignment." Shawn felt odd acknowledging out loud the likelihood that he would lose his next election but figured it would help to be as straightforward as possible.

"Oh, that's right," Becky conceded. "Well, there are lots of other causes you can help."

Becky thought for a moment, and then suggested, "How about the environment? As a Native American, the environment has always been important to me. I remember in the 1970s and '80s my grandfather used to stand by the side of the highway and tear up when he saw passersby throw trash out the window."

Shawn was starting to lose his patience. "That was a commercial!" He said this in a sharper tone than he meant to. "And the actor who played the Indian wasn't Native American, he was Italian."

"Oh, that's right. I used to watch a lot of TV," Becky continued, not allowing for time to question her clumsy excuse. "But how about the environment, don't you care about the environment?"

Shawn nodded his head. "I do."

"You're from Tulsa. Isn't there an oil pipeline in the area you could try to stop?" Becky spitballed.

It did frustrate Shawn how pipelines always seemed to be rerouted over Indian land, but it probably wasn't the best cause for him. "Oil pipelines are probably not the best cause for me. I am Osage."

Becky nodded her head in understanding, "Oh, that's right. Of course."

But Shawn could tell that Becky was pretending to understand his point.

Shawn was from one of the wealthiest families in Tulsa County. When Shawn's maternal grandfather survived a murder plot that befell the rest of his family, he inherited all the oil land his family had been killed for. The mastermind of the plot turned out to be the court-appointed financial guardian, mandated by the government to help protect the Osages from themselves. This was not an isolated incident in Tulsa at the time. Murdering entire Osage families for their oil rights turned out to be a financial windfall for many of these court appointed guardians.

When Shawn's grandfather gained back control of his family's oil rights, he invested his money over the years and became increasingly wealthy. However, Shawn knew that the foundation of his family's wealth was built on royalties from oil production, and he didn't want to do anything that Conservatives at home could label as Liberal hypocrisy. Therefore, fighting oil pipelines was out of the question.

Becky's voice perked up, "I know where you could get traction on this. This seems perfect for one of The President's anti-hate initiatives."

Shawn continued to feel deflated. "I've tried that route. I have no access to her."

But Becky persisted, "You need to go through party leadership in the House. That is the best way to get in front of The President. I know Speaker Mander very well. She is good leader, has strong medicine."

That last comment was too much for Shawn. He couldn't take any more. But he was so close to getting the access he needed for his bill. How could he turn back now? Would he be giving in to pride if he said something at this point? Or should he shut his mouth and deal with it? Compromising yourself to make deals was the job. But this was too much; Shawn felt he should say something, no matter the cost.

"Could you stop?! I can't sit here and pretend this is OK. This is completely inappropriate. What is wrong with you?" Shawn's tone was harsh, but he meant it this time.

Becky bowed her head. She looked ashamed. Shawn thought for a moment that he could see in her eyes that she felt trapped. He could sense that she wanted to scream out, *I did something really wrong, and I am sorry!*

When Becky finally replied, she looked down at the ground, "I understand your frustration. Trust me. You don't think I know what's going on? I do. I realize that you are a member of the Osage Nation, and what that means to you."

Shawn felt himself starting to forgive Becky. Maybe she carried guilt and was trying to do right. He could work with that.

Becky continued. She now lifted her gaze from the floor and looked directly into Shawn's eyes. "I realize that with my Cherokee family heritage, we haven't always seen eye to eye with the Osage. From time to time, there has been bad blood. But we must put that aside and stand together now. I am no modern-day Tecumseh … but maybe I am. And just like Tecumseh, I must unite all Native Americans … Sorry, all Liberal Native Americans. That is what I will do. Will you stand with me, brother?"

Shawn pulled out from the table and walked away.

Becky continued to shout after him as he left, "We will unite, brother! We will unite!"

Jeffery Tripp Perez

(5.0 YEARS AFTER OPPOSITE DAY DECLARED)

Jeffery got the call that confirmed his star was rising. Billie and Wilma D. wanted him to speak about the Middle East. Involvement in international politics was the last sign of leading the party on the national stage.

Moreover, the Middle East was an important topic to him. It had no direct impact on Jeffery, but he felt passionate about it. Up until now, he had always thought about his star rising on a national scale, but if he brought peace to the region, his star would not be confined to a national level, his star could rise on an international level.

Jeffery thought about the aftermath of his victory in the Middle East.

He would proudly march through the village square of the Middle East after removing the dictator, the people welcoming him and his soldiers as liberators, throwing rose petals as they stuck their heads out of windows and chanted, *libertad! libertad!* In the middle of the parade, a cute young Arab boy would bump into Jeffery when the soccer ball the boy was kicking with his friends got away from them. The boy's mother would come over to admonish the boy, yelling in a foreign language Jeffery wouldn't understand, but Jeffery understood what she was saying because he was good with context clues. He would assure the mother that there was no problem. He would tousle the little scamp's hair before lifting the child onto his shoulders and continuing the parade through the streets. At this point, the crowd would absolutely erupt.

After the parades and celebrations, elections would be held. The people would beg Jeffery to run, but his place was back home. The people would take to democracy like a fish to water. Many of the scoundrels who caused trouble in the Middle East would run for election, but the people wouldn't buy it. They would elect a well-tempered moderate, just like Jeffery.

But then, Jeffery thought, *what if they do elect one of those scoundrels?*

Jeffery then realized he was getting way ahead of himself. The first step was to inject himself into the Middle East conflict as Billie and Wilma D. had asked. After that, he could bring democracy to the country. And then, the last step would be to worry about the details of day-to-day governance.

For now, Jeffery needed to concentrate on the task at hand. Billie and Wilma D. had given him a job, and he wanted to execute it perfectly. If he was to solidify his position as a rising star, he had to impress them. He wondered what he could say that would appeal to Billie and Wilma D. Then he realized it was simple: women cared about woman stuff.

Jeffery thought back to his first election. He had spent time in Miami Beach cultivating a relationship with the gay community. When he went to gay bars for press opportunities, he noticed there were often bachelorette parties for straight women. There was nothing more annoying to Jeffery than bachelorette parties, but Miami was the bachelorette party capital of the country.

Jeffery thought about the world and the beauty of people's differences. Even though he couldn't imagine anything more annoying than a group of tiara-wearing women drunkenly screaming at the top of their lungs and carrying on with total disregard for everyone around them, he appreciated the fact that gay people loved it. More importantly, women loved gay people.

If he wanted to impress Billie and Wilma D., he would make his message about gay people and woman stuff. Jeffery called a press conference, which after his Spit Brothers press conference, received large national interest from both news outlets.

"To show solidarity with Israel," he announced, "I encourage women to hold their bachelorette parties at the Tel Aviv Pride Parade."

Jeffery knew that Tel Aviv hosted one of the largest Pride parades because clubs and restaurants in Miami often complained about the competition the week of the Tel Aviv Pride Parade. Local merchants would be annoyed at his support for Tel Aviv Pride, but that was the sacrifice he had to make as a national politician. Sometimes, local interests would have to suffer.

The press wasn't sure what the point of the press conference was, but they published his message.

Patricia Ocampo Santos (Me/Me)

(5.0 YEARS AFTER OPPOSITE DAY DECLARED)

Patricia Ocampo Santos was tasked with formulating the Liberal response to Jeffery Tripp Perez's statement. Leadership did not specifically ask her to respond, but she was the first to see the headlines and had her phone readily available. That meant the ball was in her court to craft the party's response.

If there was anything she hated more than structural racism, all police officers, non-Spanish European colonialism, and white privilege, it was Israel. Ewwww how she hated Israel. It wasn't that she hated Jews. Her partner Rory was Jewish, and he hated Israel too, so it was OK.

Before she was a politician, Patricia engaged in the most noble of professions: bartending. Because of the location of the bar where she worked, much of the bar's business was from NYU students. NYU was Jewish princess central. Patricia could always tell when they came in. They would plop down right at the bar, and it began. "It's too cold in here, can you turn up the temperature?" or, "It's too loud, can you turn down the music?" They wanted the temperature and music volume adjusted to their specific requirements, as if they were the only ones in the restaurant. And this was all before they even got their menus. Once they got their menus, that was when the entitled questions really started.

Everything was a special order or combining parts from one menu item with another. Never once did they order a dish as it was

151

offered on the menu. Then, when the food came out, they complained about how long it took, and yet they also complained that the food was under-cooked. They sent their special-ordered items back to the kitchen. There was no limit to the level of cooked something could be. The part that really frustrated Patricia was the tipping. Contrary to popular belief, they were relatively good tippers. Although, for the service they required, it was nothing special. However, the more frustrating they were, the better they would tip, as if to say, "It's OK that I behaved this way; here is some money to make it all better." That was the most insulting part of it all. Tipping was a construct of the bourgeois to keep labor subservient to capital.

This nightmare would repeat over and over again. It made her job impossible. In dealing with Israel, Patricia knew that this nuisance was no longer confined to a college bar; there was an entire country of them. Patricia shuddered. She posted:

@POS: "Instead of celebrating Pride week in a colonial state, we will arrange the largest Pride week in the Middle East outside of Israel."

Now all Patricia had to do was arrange for a Pride week celebration somewhere in the Middle East outside of Israel.

Shelly Ostrichstein (He/Him)
(5.0 YEARS AFTER OPPOSITE DAY DECLARED)

Shelly Ostrichstein was at the hospital for what should be a joyous occasion: the birth of his first grandchild. The profundity of the event was somewhat lost on Shelly though. He looked at his grandson and knew he was in trouble.

Shelly Ostrichstein was the senior Senator from New York. Shelly was an old Liberal. He lived in constant fear that younger Liberals would oust him. His only defense was to always say the most Liberal thing he could think of. He feared if he didn't, he would find himself facing a primary challenge from a younger Liberal, most likely POS.

Since the day his daughter went in for an ultrasound, Shelly knew what was coming. His daughter was having a boy. His daughter was white and Jewish. His son-in-law was white and Jewish. Still, he held out hope that there was a chance the child would be something other than a white male. *White male was no longer the right term though. It was hard to keep up with these things. What was the correct term now? Rapist!*

He loved his daughter, he loved his new grandchild, he even liked his son-in-law. But a rapist grandson was a political liability. Especially because it would be years until they had any sense of the child's sexual orientation, and Shelly faced an election sooner than that could help.

Critics said Shelly had no backbone. This couldn't be less true. In fact, doctors said that Shelly was born with too much backbone.

153

Shelly's backbone was too long for his height. It was a minor birth defect with no medical consequences, but it left a crevasse between Shelly's neck and shoulders. When Shelly needed to escape, he relaxed his neck, placing his head further down into the crevasse. This was his safe space, where he did his best thinking.

On the way to his New York office, Shelly saw a small fire in the lobby of the building next door. He was initially concerned, but then saw that bystanders were on the phone, likely calling the fire department. Shelly figured he couldn't do anything to help and made his way to his office.

He was hosting Israel's top diplomat and had to get ready for the meeting.

Zvi Yarokin

(5.0 YEARS AFTER OPPOSITE DAY DECLARED)

Zvi Yarokin, Israeli Diplomat, landed in New York. On orders from the Prime Minister, he was to go straight from the airport to Senator Ostrichstein's office. Zvi was on a special mission: he was here to find out why Americans couldn't stand Israel anymore.

Once he was off the plane, Zvi went with the other passengers to immigration and passport control. When he got to where the line started, he became impatient.

Zvi hated lines. Back home, he was not alone in this. Everyone in Israel hated lines. Every other country must have loved lines, because whenever Zvi traveled abroad, he ended up in lines. Lines in Israel meant that whoever was in the biggest rush pushed their way to the front. If someone didn't want you to cut them, they would give you a light shove, and that would be the end of it. You would impatiently wait behind them.

Zvi had some time before his meeting with the Senator, but he couldn't just stand in this line. It was unbearable. Zvi made his way to the side of the line where there was some room to pass and began to walk past people ahead of him. Occasionally, someone threw up their arms in frustration, or said *hey!* But no one lightly pushed him. If they lightly pushed him, Zvi would know that he could cut no further.

Zvi got out of the airport in record time. He found his driver and was on his way. Record time!

Zvi made it to the Senator's office with a few hours to spare. He figured he would walk around the area and get a sense of how people on the street felt before talking to the Senator. Zvi's conversations confirmed his fears. Everywhere he went, he sensed palpable hostility towards Israel; everyone he interacted with seemed angry with him. A waitress at a diner yelled at him for trying to haggle with her on the price of items on the menu. It was her loss— Zvi's cousin owned a cell phone store in the area, and Zvi had offered her a great deal in return. A man on the street cursed at Zvi when Zvi answered his phone while the man was giving him directions. What was Zvi supposed to do, let the call go to voicemail? No one in Israel had voicemail. Every call was picked up as it was received.

Finally, it was time to go to the Senator's office. Zvi had trouble getting into the lobby. The street was jammed with fire trucks. There looked to be a serious fire in the building next door. When he entered the lobby, he sensed more hostility. As he passed people waiting in the security line to check in, he heard some of them cursing at him. No one lightly shoved him, which meant they weren't upset about him cutting the line. They must have been opponents of Israel and known that he was here to see the Senator.

Shelly Ostrichstein (He/Him) & Zvi Yarokin

(5.0 YEARS AFTER OPPOSITE DAY DECLARED)

Just as Zvi and Shelly sat down to meet, there was an announcement over the building's intercom: "This is not a drill. All occupants, please make your way to the nearest exit. I repeat, this is not a drill."

Shelly was quick to assure Zvi, "Don't worry about that. It's fine. We get those messages all the time. How was your flight in?"

Zvi was not fully convinced it was fine. "Are you sure? I saw the fire in the building next door. It looked serious."

"Yes, we go through this all the time, it's completely normal. Don't worry about it." Shelly sounded frustrated that Zvi was not appeased by his previous assurance.

Shelly then pressed the intercom to speak to his staff in the rest of his office. He repeated to them not to be concerned, there was nothing to worry about. They should all go about their business.

Zvi and Shelly had met a few times over the years. Shelly was an outspoken supporter of Israel earlier in his career, but after Opposite Day was declared, he became conspicuously silent on the topic. At the same time, Israel became increasingly unpopular with Liberals.

Zvi wanted to know how Shelly could remain silent as a leading member of the Liberal Party. Zvi was trained in the art of Israeli diplomacy. He got right to the point. "Why do Liberals hate Israel? How could you let this happen? You say nothing. They hate Israel more and more by the day."

At that moment, the sound of Middle Eastern dance music began blaring from Zvi's pocket. Both Shelly and Zvi sat silently for a moment.

"Oh sorry, is that me?" Zvi said as he reached for his phone, "It's a very popular ringtone in Israel. I thought it might be you."

Zvi picked up the phone. "Zvi Yarokin, Israeli Diplomat. Yes, I can talk. No … no … yes … OK, OK, OK. This is no problem. OK. Goodbye."

Zvi hung up the phone. He saw that the senator looked visibly frustrated. His point about Liberals and Israel must have resonated.

Shelly could tell that Zvi was on edge. Come to think of it, Zvi had seemed on edge every time Shelly had seen him. Shelly would do his best to calm him down. "Zvi, I assure you that Liberals don't hate Israel. Sure, they dislike some of your policies, but they don't hate the country or the people. Your assessment is not fair."

Zvi heard a commotion outside the office from the senator's staff. The room was getting warmer. Zvi could smell the smoke. It was potent. Zvi heard more fire engines blaring on the streets below. He wondered how bad the situation was.

"You seem delusional," Zvi shot back at Shelly with a textbook nuanced move used in Israeli diplomacy. "It's not our policies, they don't want us to exist."

Shelly became increasingly frustrated. "Well, it's not like you've tried to make peace in recent years."

"What's to make peace?" Zvi replied. "How do you make peace when they don't want you to exist? It's not about land or occupation. I know from my time in Mossad there is no one in their government that can offer peace. They won't accept our presence. Our existence is an affront to them."

Zvi was never in the Mossad. Because of conscription laws in Israel, all citizens served in the army. Mossad was the Israeli intelligence agency: the most elite unit in which one could serve. For the last few decades, Israel was going through severe Mossad inflation. Roughly 30 percent of Israeli men claimed to be members or former members of Mossad.

Shelly was well aware that Zvi had never served in the Mossad. Shelly lived in New York in the 1990s. He witnessed the same phenomenon with cab drivers. For some reason, 20 percent of New York cab drivers in the 1990s claimed to be the former Surgeon General of India. Or, if not the Surgeon General, then a very prominent brain surgeon. Like most New Yorkers at the time, Shelly believed that he had ridden in the cab of at least five former Surgeon Generals of India. It was on the sixth time he heard this story that Shelly realized some of these men were exaggerating their backgrounds.

Shelly realized that Zvi was starting to grate on him. Why couldn't Zvi just accept his assurances? "You still have the full support of the Liberal Party. I am telling you, it's not like Liberals are being co-opted by internal forces that oppose the very existence of a Jewish State. It's just your policies. That's it."

Zvi and the senator were interrupted by the sound of knocking. It was one of the senator's aides. "Um sir, there are firemen in the office. They say we need to evacuate."

"Fire*fighters*!" Shelly corrected impatiently.

"Yes, sorry," the aide said as quickly as possible. "The fire*fighters* say we need to evacuate."

At that moment, a firefighter burst through the door of the senator's office, unwilling to wait for the aide to convince the senator. The firefighter was furious. "What are you doing here? Are you crazy? Do you not see the smoke? You need to evacuate the building now!"

Shelly sank his head lower into his safe space. He then lifted his head and said, "Excuse me. We are in the middle of a very important meeting. Thank you for your concern, but we are fine."

Shelly then addressed his aide, "I understand your concern, but I assure you there is nothing to worry about. The fire was clearly in the building next door. It is not after this building. It only wants the building next door. Go back to work. Everything will be fine."

The firefighter was in a state of disbelief. "I don't have time for this. If you stay, it's your funeral."

The firefighter ran out the door. The aide looked scared but went back to convey the Senator's message that all was well.

Shelly turned his focus back to Zvi and calmly said, "Sorry about that. Where were we?"

Zvi was no longer comfortable with Shelly's assurances. "I really think we should leave. There was smoke in the halls when they opened the doors."

Shelly couldn't understand why Zvi wouldn't accept his assurances. He was in the building too. It's not like he would ever allow them to be in any real danger. "It's fine, trust me," Shelly said.

Zvi decided to put his concerns aside and get back to the meeting. "OK. You say we should enter peace talks. Why should we be the ones to make peace? 'He Started It.'"

Shelly unbuttoned the top button of his shirt and loosened his tie. It was getting uncomfortably hot in the room. Shelly just had someone in the office to fix the air conditioning, so he wasn't sure why he was sweating, but he would have time to deal with that later. Zvi had just used the argument he was waiting for. "Well, you say 'He Started It,' but in your conflict with the Liberals, you started it. So why should Liberals believe you regarding who started what?"

Zvi knew the senator had a point. Israel's Prime Minister had come to the U.S. and openly campaigned against The Former$^{\wedge 3}$ President 10 years ago. When The Former$^{\wedge 3}$ President predictably won reelection, Israel was on the outs with Liberals. It didn't matter what the Liberals did before, openly campaigning against the president of your biggest ally was the nuclear option, and it failed.

Zvi put his hands in the air with his palms facing Shelly and said in a chastened manner, "I know, I know, I know. But how long can you hold a grudge?" Zvi then put his hands down and continued, "This isn't just politics anymore. The antisemites have real power in your party. I understand you are in a precarious position, but you must speak up. Say something. What's another six years of power if they march your children to the gas chambers in eight?"

Shelly began coughing, which was odd, because it wasn't allergy season, but he was having trouble breathing. Shelly then realized what was going on. The air conditioning wasn't broken, and he wasn't having an allergy attack; Shelly was coming down with something.

"You are completely overreacting. Everything is fine. Just because people in the party disagree with Israel's policies doesn't mean they are antisemitic." Shelly paused for a moment to cough, it was getting harder to breathe. Shelly thought it was odd how quickly this cold was hitting him. Maybe he had been sick for a while and didn't realize it. He continued, "Whenever anyone in the party speaks out against Israel, they make sure to say they are speaking out against the Israeli government or its policies. Why would they say they are against Israel's government or policies if they really meant they hated Israel, and deep down, all Jews? Wouldn't they just say that instead? Think about it. You are making no sense."

Smoke billowed through the door. The fire had clearly made it up to their floor. Zvi rose out of his chair. "We must go now. This fire is bad."

Shelly couldn't stand it anymore. He felt hot, sick, and couldn't breathe. On top of all that, Zvi was so frustrating. And this nonsense about the fire next door. Shelly stood up and slammed his hands on the table and yelled, "There is no fire!"

When Shelly stood up to yell, he took a deep breath. He was overcome by the smoke in the room. He began to choke and cough more violently. He looked over at Zvi, "Oh, I see it now. That's not good." Shelly fell back in his chair. He tried to sink his head into his safe place, but he couldn't muster the strength. He then passed out in his chair.

Zvi sprang over the desk to where Shelly was slumped in his chair. He grabbed Shelly's body and threw him over his shoulders. While Zvi had never been a member of the Mossad, he did complete his army service with the Search and Rescue Brigade. He rushed out of Shelly's office with the senator draped over his shoulders. He searched for staffers and found the loyal few who had stayed behind on the senator's orders. He led them out of the office and down the stairs. On their way down, they found several workers from other offices who were trapped in the fire. Zvi brought them into the group and led them all downstairs. He safely delivered the group of people through the lobby and onto the street, out of the burning building.

When he got down to the street, paramedics and firefighters were waiting for them. There was no one left in the building. Zvi had found and brought down the last 10 people who were trapped. After a while, members of the group Zvi saved told the story of how he had gotten them out. The story made its way around to the emergency responders.

The captain of the fire department came over to Zvi and shook his hand. "What you did in there was incredible," the fire captain said, making no attempt to hide the reverence in his voice.

Zvi saw the admiration in the fire captain's eyes. *A friendly face?* Zvi wondered. Zvi's training in the art of Israeli diplomacy had prepared him for all kinds of situations: peace treaties, cease fires, hostage negotiations, second peace treaties, prisoner exchanges, third peace treaties. But nothing in his training prepared him for this situation. Zvi would have to wing it; he was in unchartered territory. "Of course, this was no problem. I saw that your guys could not do it, so I helped. It was easy for me."

Zvi looked over at his new friend but saw that the admiration on the fire captain's face had been replaced by a more familiar look. The fire captain was visibly angry when Zvi talked. Zvi knew it was his Israeli accent that set him off. He couldn't figure out why there was so much animosity towards Israel from everyone he spoke with.

Suddenly, Middle Eastern dance music began to blare from Zvi's pocket. Zvi picked up his phone. "Zvi Yarokin, Israeli diplomat. Yes … yes … of course … no …"

By the time Zvi got off the phone, the fire captain was walking away and waving his hands in the air in frustration. Zvi knew he had to fix the anti-Israel sentiment he was finding everywhere he went.

He had no time for the fire captain anyway. He was meeting with Liberal Party leadership. He would have to turn on his charm if he wanted them to abandon their Middle East Pride Parade plans. It would take every bit of Israeli diplomacy Zvi could muster.

Rory Cohen (It/It)

(5.0 YEARS AFTER OPPOSITE DAY DECLARED)

Immediately after meeting with Zvi, Liberal Party leadership decided to move forward with the Middle East Pride Parade. Coordination of the parade was delegated to Rory Cohen. Leadership figured since Rory was Jewish and disliked Israel, it was OK. The parade was nearly good to go, but there were two problems. They couldn't find a country in the Middle East other than Israel willing to host a Pride parade, and they couldn't find members of the LGBTQ community willing to go to a Pride parade in a Middle Eastern country other than Israel. Besides these two issues, everything else for the parade was set to go.

The second problem was a source of frustration for Liberal Party leadership. The LGBTQ community were vocal advocates in the 'He Started It' wars and firmly believed Israel started it.

While Liberal Party leadership was increasingly frustrated, Rory was not concerned. He did not fight for the parade in the same dogged manner that his opponents had become accustomed to. Some speculated that he was going soft. Others attributed it to a possible personal health concern. In the past few weeks, Rory had been walking with a limp. One day he brought in a cane. He never directly addressed the issue, but it was clear that he could no longer walk without it.

As the target date for the parade approached, it became clear that there was still no country willing to host, and potential attendees refused to commit. Rory still seemed unfazed. The Party stopped promoting the parade, and eventually suspended its plans.

The Middle East Pride Parade did not flounder because of Conservative opposition, it died from apathy within the ranks of the Liberal Party. But a Pride Parade in a Middle Eastern country other than Israel was such a good idea, apathy alone was not enough to kill it. This must have been the work of subversives from within the Party, Rory concluded.

Agitators from within the Party had been a top concern for Rory and Patricia ever since they imagined their society of equality.

When Liberals won their majority in the wake of the Alpha-Alpha strain, there was so much in front of them to accomplish. They had two years to push through everything they had ever wanted. They would reshape society—it was their moral duty. Without Conservative opposition, they were finally free to do so.

But even after the roadblock of Conservative opposition collapsed, their goals remained elusive. Where they once found opposition, a new enemy emerged. At first, the new enemy seemed like a minor hiccup they could easily overcome. But unlike party opposition, this enemy was insidious. It did not state it was an enemy, it pretended to be a friend. It wasn't clear it was an enemy until it was too late. Where Patricia and Rory once faced opposition, they now faced compromise.

Compromise!!! Compromise was not always bad. Sometimes it was needed to get things done in a practical manner. But, on questions of morality, it was unacceptable. Patricia and Rory were always driven by morality.

Their war on Conservative opposition was a war against a foreign army. It was clear who was their friend and who was their enemy. Their war on compromise would not be against an opposing foreign force; it would be a civil war.

Civil wars are fought with less civility than foreign wars. Most foreign wars involve practical differences that cannot be resolved without bloodshed. Civil wars involve fundamental differences that cannot be resolved without total destruction. The most vicious of these conflicts involve a root of betrayal. Betrayal at the heart of a conflict is the most serious of all offenses. Betrayal does not necessitate the total destruction of an enemy; instead, their destruction is a joyous byproduct of the battle. This was a civil war that involved betrayal.

To combat this insidious enemy from within, Patricia, Rory and the Davids created the House Unkind Activities Committee, or HUAC for short. They had the blessing of leadership to combat all members who stood in the way of reshaping society. To ensure that everyone on HUAC thought as they thought and believed in what they believed in, Patricia filled the committee with her best friends in the whole world: members of "The Posse".

6.0 YEARS AFTER OPPOSITE DAY DECLARED

Geraldine Mander (She/Her)

Geraldine Mander was not fucking around. She was Speaker of the House. She rose through the ranks of the party because she knew where all the bodies were buried. She spent most of her career burying those bodies. She was not fucking around.

Through her career, Geraldine saw many POSes come and go. But Patricia Ocampo Santos proved harder to control than she expected. Geraldine knew when to fight and when to let a potential threat punch themselves into exhaustion. She decided to let Patricia hang herself, but it was taking longer than expected.

Party leadership instructed Geraldine to go along with HUAC. When the committee brought her names of party members, she would bring a vote to have them stripped of their committee assignments. All they needed was a majority vote, but majorities were for wimps. Geraldine would get all the votes in her party inline. Once the members were stripped of their committee assignments, their time in Congress was up. They would be useless until the next election, when voters would switch them out for someone who could be useful in office.

Since party leadership told her to go along with HUAC, she would. Everyone has a boss. And anyone who didn't go along with her votes would be another body to bury.

Shawn Bennet

(6.0 YEARS AFTER OPPOSITE DAY DECLARED)

Shawn Bennet sat in on the first HUAC hearings, even though he didn't want to be there. He knew that HUAC was bad for him, but that didn't matter much. He had to be there.

Shawn had been desperate to make some headway on his legislation protecting senior citizens from fraud. He had almost given up when he was approached by Rex Kellermam, The President's most trusted and loyal advisor. Rex informed Shawn that The President would be interested in meeting with him about his proposed legislation in the near future. Rex then spent several minutes asking Shawn security vetting questions.

This was the first promising turn for Shawn's legislation. For the first time since he had come to Washington, Shawn felt a sense of hope. But the hope came at a price. Shawn now had something to lose, which meant there was something to hold over him. He could not afford to rock the boat. So, Shawn attended the hearings because all Liberal Party members were asked to attend. Now that his legislation had some hope, he had to avoid the wrath of HUAC, who had their sights set on members from The Walking Dead.

POS was in her element at the hearing. It was impressive; she really knew how to take someone down. On the first day of hearings, she called up Molly Cutler, a member of The Walking Dead from Iowa's 4th District, a solidly Conservative stronghold. Molly was elected because the 4th District, like Tulsa, was a place where Conservatives took to spitting directly into each other's mouths during the Alpha-Alpha outbreak.

Molly ran afoul of Patricia and The Posse on a spending bill. Patricia and The Posse attempted to pass a spending bill that would double the funding for Taco Tuesday. Molly was desperate to show her worth to her district and tried to tack a rider onto the bill enforcing the use of domestically grown corn for all Taco Tuesday celebrations. However, after considering the issue, Patricia determined that using domestically grown corn for Taco Tuesday was in fact a form of cultural appropriation.

Patricia Ocampo Santos (Me/Me)
(6.0 YEARS AFTER OPPOSITE DAY DECLARED)

Molly's attempted appropriation of Taco Tuesday was unforgivable. Patricia knew she couldn't bring Molly up for a violation involving Taco Tuesday though, because any fight involving Taco Tuesday risked highlighting its increasing budgetary needs and could call the entire institution into question. But Molly still had to pay.

For too long, Patricia's social programs were met with budgetary constraints, while everything benefiting farmers in Molly's district was passed right away. Patricia knew she had enough to hang Molly. She would make quick work of her.

Patricia Began her questioning of Molly Cutler at the first HUAC hearing. "You say you have always been a member of the Liberal Party, is that right?"

"That is correct. A Liberal through and through," Molly replied with a nervous cheeriness.

"That must have been hard, growing up in such a Conservative district," Patricia asked with an overtly feigned commiseration.

Molly tried to shrug off Patricia's goading. "People were pretty accepting. It used to not be a big deal."

Patricia now feigned a sense of relief. "Oh, that's nice. It's heartwarming to see white people accept other whites."

Molly picked her head up and said, "Excuse me?"

Patricia sensed she may have gone too far, and decided it was time to get Molly on the defensive. "Sorry, that was unrelated. But you say that your peers growing up were accepting of your Liberal beliefs. Are you now or have you ever been a member of a non-Liberal Party?"

"I'm not sure what you mean. I have been a loyal member of the party my entire life." Molly found herself becoming a mixture of angry and defensive. "And it's not like I was loyal from the comfort of a solidly Liberal district. I had to take a stand for what I believe in, even though it wasn't popular with my peers."

Now that Patricia had Molly on the defensive, she knew that Molly was toast. "Could it be that your peers accepted your Liberal beliefs because they knew you weren't really a Liberal at heart?"

Molly became indignant. "For the last time, no. I've been a loyal member of the party. I have not engaged in non-Liberal activities."

Patricia was about to expose Molly for the closet Conservative she was. "Can you explain these photos then?"

Patricia projected pictures of Molly onto a large TV screen. Many of the Liberals in the crowd, led by Patricia's Posse, gasped at what they saw.

Molly had a confused look on her face when she saw the pictures. "Sorry, where did you get those pictures?" The indignity that was previously in Molly's voice turned to confusion.

Patricia ignored Molly's question and pressed on with questions of her own. "Is that you in the photos?"

"Yes, of course it's me," Molly said still in a confused state. "Those are from my wedding. I just have no idea where you got my wedding photos or how they are relevant to this committee."

Patricia couldn't believe Molly so readily admitted it. Shouldn't she be ashamed of her monstrous ways? Perhaps this could be a teachable moment. But the time for teachable moments had passed. Now was the time for retribution. "So, you admit that this is you in your wedding photos?"

"Of course." The confusion in Molly's voice was becoming more pronounced. "What does this have to do with anything?"

Patricia again ignored Molly's question and continued with her own. "Well, where was your wedding held?"

"I don't understand the relevance," Molly said, half protesting.

"Just answer the question," Patricia snapped. "The quicker you answer, the sooner this will be over."

"Fine. The wedding was, of course, in my district in Iowa," Molly conceded.

Patricia rolled her eyes, trying to give the sense that Molly was being evasive in her answer. "I meant, where in your district? What was the venue?"

"We held the service in our local church. Then we had our reception at a local catering hall," Molly answered.

Patricia then followed up, "And this church and catering hall, these were both indoors?"

"Yes," Molly said impatiently.

Patricia had Molly just where she wanted her. She would now prove to the world as well as to Molly, what a monster Molly was. "So, here you are in your wedding photos … maskless, at an indoor wedding."

The revelation did little to alleviate Molly's confusion. "Huh? This was 15 years ago, well before the pandemic. Why would we wear masks?"

Patricia looked blankly at Molly. She was glad she decided to hold Molly accountable and not make this a teachable moment. Molly was too far gone to be saved. "Well, we are supposed to wear masks now." Patricia said matter-of-factly.

"But this was 15 years ago. There was no pandemic. Why would we wear masks?" Molly was only more confused after Patricia's revelation.

"Yes, you have mentioned that," Patricia said, acknowledging one of Molly's questions for the first time. "But you know that it is a Liberal Party rule to wear masks at all indoor events, don't you? Especially when there are cameras."

"Yes, and I always do," Molly said.

"But you didn't back then?" Patricia half questioned.

"It wasn't a rule back then." Molly was becoming exasperated.

Patricia couldn't believe Molly's continued confusion. Patricia had spelled it out for her, and still Molly didn't get what a Conservative monster she was. "But it's a commonly held practice today. By today's standards, wouldn't you consider your actions to be non-Liberal, even subversive?"

"But it wasn't a common practice at all back then," Molly insisted.

"But it is now! Should you not be held accountable for propagating the backwards and regressive policies of a previous period?" Patricia shot back.

Molly rolled her eyes, "This is silly."

"Well, I'm sorry you consider this silly. But just because a regressive policy was commonplace in the past does not make your complicity in its propagation acceptable to me. Maybe it does to some half-hearted Liberals out there. But I must take a stand against your subversive actions." Patricia felt she really had to drive her point home. Not for the members of the committee, who clearly knew right from wrong, but for poor Molly, who didn't know enough to know she had done wrong. Patricia caught herself. She was too forgiving. That was her weakness. Patricia had to remind herself, *they were past the point of teachable moments, this was retribution.* "For me and other true believers, it doesn't matter if it happened two weeks, two years, or even two decades ago. A thoughtless act is a thoughtless act. To me, you are guilty of a thoughtless crime."

"Thoughtless crime?" Molly had never heard the term before, but she knew it made her uncomfortable.

Patricia couldn't believe she had to spell it out to this degree for Molly. "Yes, thoughtless crime. Anything that would be considered a thoughtless action today should be considered a thoughtless action in any time period. And your actions here are enough to prove that you are guilty of thoughtless crime." Patricia was certain that Molly would be racked with guilt now that Patricia had laid bare Molly's reprehensible behavior, but she had to press forward. "But thoughtless crime isn't your only subversive action," Patricia continued.

Molly shook her head, shrugged her shoulders, and lifted her hands in the air. "What do you think I did now?"

"Well, your voting record. You say you are a loyal member of the Liberal Party, but your voting record says otherwise," Patricia said.

Molly nearly stood up from her seat. She couldn't believe what she was hearing. "What do you mean? I have voted for every one of your spending bills. No matter how crazy they seemed."

Patricia fell back in her chair, as though Molly's assertion physically knocked her back. "Crazy? What do you mean crazy?"

Molly was unfazed by Patricia's physical show of aghast disbelief. "All of your vague social and environmental justice spending bills. I voted for each one of them. How is my voting record not Liberal enough?"

Patricia recovered in her chair. She didn't care how petty Molly got; she had the courage to power through this battle. "Well, that is true, you voted for each spending bill the party has put forward. But it's also about what you proposed."

The confused look returned to Molly's face, "I have no idea what you're talking about."

Patricia closed her eyes so as to fight back the emotions of the moment. "Since you have been in Congress, you've tried to introduce three separate spending proposals. Each of them aimed at subsidizing farmers and none of them promoting social justice in the inner cities."

"Well, yes, I am from Iowa, that is who I represent." Molly realized her tone was becoming sarcastic and she didn't want to antagonize Patricia, so she followed up with, "That hasn't stopped me from supporting all bills in support of spending for inner city social justice." However, when Molly finished her comment, she could tell that

Patricia had already moved on. Patricia was looking past Molly, to the other members of Congress now when she spoke.

Patricia was done with Molly. She had shown the committee and the other members of Congress the type of monster that lurked in her party and dared to call herself friend. She now looked past Molly and even past the other members of Congress who sat behind Molly, to the TV cameras placed at the back of the room. This message was for the people. "But every stalk of corn that is subsidized could have been another tax credit for an electric car. Every soybean that receives government funding could have been money to support environmental justice agents. Every unneeded bale of wheat could have been a subsidy for offshore wind farms, which would provide power intermittently. That is what I see when I see your spending proposals."

Molly had again moved from confusion to indignance, "So, what should I do? Should I not represent the interest of my constituents? Do you propose that we stop supporting the farms, which are the backbone and lifeblood of this country?"

Patricia looked at Molly as though she had been waiting to hear this question. "You say farms are the backbone and lifeblood of this country, but I say your farms rest on the broad shoulders of the inner cities. Burn down your farms and leave our cities, and our cities will live on agricultural imports from abroad. But burn down our cities, and dust will settle on every farm across the country for want of subsidies from our cities. And while I recognize that you must support the best interests of your constituents, I argue that they do not know their best interests. And I cannot and will not stand idly by and remain complicit as you attempt to nail our social agenda to a cross made of corn."

Shawn Bennet

(6.0 YEARS AFTER OPPOSITE DAY DECLARED)

Frank Vultaggio looked over at Shawn as they sat and watched the hearings and said, "Jeez. This is nuts."

Shawn shook his head, "Yeah, it's no joke." Shawn then became visibly frustrated. "They expect us to vote to have everyone stripped of their committee assignments? I'm not doing it."

Frank chuckled. Shawn's naivety still caught him off guard. "I don't think it matters which way you vote. They have the votes. And if you don't vote their way, you'll just be next in front of the committee."

"I'm not doing it." Shawn had no intention of relenting. "Have you even heard from the committee yet?"

Frank shook his head. "No, not yet. The jobs number comes out later this week. My guess is that senior members convinced POS to hold off on subpoenaing me until I give them my read on the report later this week. Those greedy fucks."

"I haven't heard from the committee yet either. I'm surprised," Shawn said.

HUAC had already subpoenaed all members of The Walking Dead other than Frank and Shawn. Frank and Shawn watched the committee meeting day after day. There was nothing they could do as their peers were paraded in front of the committee. One by one, each was accused of thoughtless crime. Then POS would ask them the question, "Are you now or have you ever been a member of a non-Liberal Party?"

When the defendants realized the pattern of accusation and that denial was futile, they took the Fifth Amendment. But Patricia just labeled them Fifth Amendment Conservatives, and HUAC found them guilty of subversion.

Later in the week, Frank held his meeting to discuss the likely outcome of the jobs report. He told the members that the analyst from the National Bureau of Labor Statistics looked terrible when he saw him on the street, which meant the jobs number would be bad. It was a sure thing. Frank recommended they buy the market before the number came out. It was his strongest conviction yet.

Immediately after the meeting, Frank received his subpocna from HUAC.

Shawn couldn't contain his disgust. They didn't even wait a few days after the meeting to pretend they had some common decency. Once they had what they wanted from Frank, they subpoenaed him. Now Shawn was angry.

Shawn sat alone during Frank's hearing. All other members of The Walking Dead had been found guilty of subversion by HUAC. Their names were submitted to Geraldine Mander. The vote to strip the members of their committee assignments was the next day. But first, HUAC would pass judgement on Frank Vultaggio. Once he was convicted, House Speaker Mander would hold the vote for the six members of The Walking Dead at the same time.

Shawn still hadn't heard from the committee. He couldn't figure out why.

Patricia called Frank's hearing to order and got right to the point. "Are you now or have you ever been a member of a non-Liberal Party?"

Frank rolled his eyes in a manner that was more indicative of boredom than disbelief. He then leaned forward and said, "I invoke my constitutional right to tell you to blow it out of your ass."

Patricia was not taken aback by Frank's comment. She was not surprised that Frank would stoop to such a vulgar and base reaction. "Excuse me?" She feigned surprise.

Frank bent further down, so as to speak more clearly into the microphone on the table in front of him. "I invoke my constitutional right to tell you to blow it out of your ass."

Rory Cohen, who was now confined to a wheelchair, tried to lift himself up to object, but could not. "We object!!!" he shouted.

Frank laughed as he looked over at Rory. "What's wrong, Rory? Has POS been stepping on your balls too much? Can't get out of your chair? Yeah, I know about that."

Rory's medical condition was in fact the result of his relationship with Patricia. Their activities were taking a physical toll on him.

Patricia stood up. She knew that Frank was a troglodyte, but she couldn't imagine he would stoop to this vulgar an accusation. Before she realized what she was saying, she yelled, "I would never engage in a relationship with a Jew ... I mean subordinate. Sorry, I meant subordinate."

The members of Congress stood in stunned silence as Rory quickly called for a recess. Patricia huddled with Rory for a few moments, then Patricia came back and addressed the chamber. "I would like to apologize for my comments. It was a slip of the tongue. I am truly sorry to anyone who was offended. I condemn all forms of antisemitism ... and Islamophobia."

Patricia was immediately forgiven. She then turned back to questioning Frank. "Sorry for the interruption. Are you now or have you ever been a member of a non-Liberal Party?"

Frank bent down again to speak clearly into the microphone and said, "I ain't telling you nothing. So, whatever you ask me, I will invoke my constitutional right to tell you to blow it out of your ass."

The chamber sat in stunned silence. Shawn bit his lip. He had been trying not to laugh, but Frank's response got better every time he heard it. After Frank's last response, Shawn couldn't contain himself any longer, and he burst out laughing.

Shawn's laughter echoed through the halls of Congress, the contrasting silence of the room amplifying the sound more than Shawn had anticipated. But Shawn didn't care. Even if it jeopardized his bill and brought the wrath of HUAC down on him he didn't care. He now laughed with total disregard for what others thought.

The members of HUAC did not see the humor. They cited Frank for contempt, escorted him out of the room, and found him guilty in absentia.

Now, Geraldine Mander had all the names she needed to put up for a vote the next day.

As the Representatives shuffled out of the chamber, Shawn was stopped by an aide to Speaker Mander, who said the Speaker would like to talk to him.

Ted Cruise

Volvo 140, Volvo 164, Volvo 200 Series, Volvo 300 Series, Volvo 700 Series, Volvo 850 Series, Volvo S40, and Volvo 870... Alfa Romeo 75, Alfa Romeo 33, Alfa Romeo 155, Alfa Romeo 156, Alfa Romeo Alfasud, Alfa Romeo Arna, Alfa Romeo Brera ....

Shawn Bennet, Geraldine Mander, and Asher Mander

(6.0 Years after Opposite Day Declared)

hen Shawn got to Geraldine Mander's office, she looked stone-faced and emotionless. Shawn was told that was how she looked when she was angry. She always looked stone-faced and emotionless.

When Shawn walked in, Geraldine greeted him coldly. "Representative Bennet, thank you for coming.

Shawn tried to get out a reply, "Of course…" but Geraldine interrupted him before he could respond further.

Geraldine was uninterested in his small talk. "Isn't that wonderful," she said in a way that Shawn sensed she would have responded to anything he said. "I couldn't help but notice you were laughing today at Representative Vultaggio's antics."

Shawn decided he would play this contrite, but not too contrite. "Yes. Sorry, he just cracks me up I guess."

Geraldine began speaking before Shawn could fully finish his sentence. Shawn felt again as though Geraldine would have responded in this manner no matter what he said. "Yes, I don't care about that. Frankly, I don't care about why or when you laugh. This isn't grade school. What I do care about is your dedication to our cause. You have a significant vote tomorrow. We have the votes with or without you. But you will vote with the party, of course."

Shawn was nervous. He thought about his proposed legislation and the senior citizens he wanted to protect. He had determined after his meeting with Becky Werner how far he would go in order to get some traction on his legislation. Shawn figured he was willing to take a passive role in some of the backwards behavior he saw by not actively standing up to it. But this was different. By asking him to vote against Frank and the other members of The Walking Dead, they were asking Shawn to take a more active role in this perverse behavior.

"Well actually, I haven't yet decided." Shawn was lying. He had no intention of voting against the other members of The Walking Dead. But he was too nervous to tell Geraldine to her face.

Geraldine looked stone-faced and emotionless. Shawn could tell she was pissed.

"Oh, I see," Geraldine said, "Well, I must say that's an interesting answer. I think party leadership would be very interested to hear it." Geraldine's tone was not threatening. In a way, that made it more threatening to Shawn, as though he was so insignificant to her that she didn't have to bother threatening him.

Shawn was also confused by Geraldine's statement. What did she mean, *what party leadership thought*? Didn't she know what she thought? "I'm sorry, aren't I talking to party leadership?" Shawn asked.

"Ha!" Geraldine laughed, not in the way someone laughs at a funny joke, but in a way an adult laughs when a young child says or does something cute. "Young man, you are charming."

A chubby teenager walked into the room; his face buried in a portable video game console. Shawn guessed he was about 15 years old. However, that might be wrong, because he had tattoos up his right arm.

Shawn figured the teen was at the office with a member of Geraldine's staff and accidentally wandered into her office.

The teenager walked behind Geraldine's desk without picking his head up from his video game. When he reached her chair, she stood up and he sat down. Geraldine walked towards the door. As she got to the door, she looked back at the teenager and said, "Asher, honey ... I'm sorry."

The teen then impatiently shot back at her, "Grandma!!! I think you've done enough. Just close the door behind you."

Asher Mander picked his head up from his video game, looked at Shawn, and said, "You are a terrible person."

Shawn had no idea what was going on. "Huh?" was the only reaction he could muster.

Asher then elaborated on his original statement. "You are a terrible person. I am a much better person than you."

Shawn still had no clue what was going on. "What are you talking about? Who are you?"

"Party leadership," Asher responded bluntly.

Shawn was only more confused. "What are you talking about? You can't even vote. How are you party leadership?"

"The party has empowered my generation," Asher explained. "They recognize how corrupt older generations are. You are destroying the planet, propagating hate, and keeping us in the dark ages. My generation is here to lead the world into the future."

Shawn rolled his eyes, "Who the hell are you? What have you done that is so great? There is no way you can be leadership."

Shawn looked at Asher. The moment Shawn started speaking, Asher placed his phone upright on the table, pointing the camera back at himself. Asher then started dancing. Shawn stopped speaking when he saw Asher dancing, which went on for about a minute or so. Asher then picked up his phone, pressed a few buttons and looked back at Shawn. "Sorry, what were you saying?"

Shawn gave up on his last point. He just wanted to get out of there. Talking to Asher was a waste of his time. "What do you even want?" Shawn asked.

"Your vote tomorrow," Asher said matter-of-factly. "All we ask is that you do the right thing."

Shawn put his foot down. He was intimidated by Geraldine, but he wouldn't hold back from a teenager. "No way I am voting with the party tomorrow."

Asher smirked. "You don't think we have anything on you? You haven't committed any thoughtless crimes?" Asher asked rhetorically. "You are wrong. The only reason you weren't hauled before the committee like the rest of your ancient regressive cronies is because we didn't like the optics of prosecuting one of the most diverse members of Congress. But make no mistake, if you cross us, we will do it in a heartbeat."

Unlike Geraldine, Asher did feel the need to threaten Shawn. Whereas the absence of a threat made Shawn feel threatened from Geraldine, the presence of threats from Asher made Shawn feel emboldened.

"What do I care? Either way, I am gone in a year," Shawn scoffed, not concerned by the growing contempt in his voice.

"You think it's over once you're out of here? This will follow you." Asher was not done with his threats. "We will follow you. I am the leader of the future. Once you've been deemed a hateful monster, you, your children, and their children will never be able to wash off the stink. Your thoughtless crime will follow you around. Stories of your hatefulness will ring through the generations. It will be part of school curricula. Righting the wrongs of the past only gets us halfway there. The wrongs of the past must be avenged!"

Shawn wanted to leave, but he was sort of having fun watching Asher get upset. "The only thing I have done since I got here is try to stop people from scamming senior citizens. You don't have anything on me," Shawn said, knowing this would drive Asher nuts.

Asher's eyes opened wide. He looked as surprised as he was angry. As though he couldn't believe that Shawn would not roll over. "Oh really?" Asher's voice was almost shaking. "What about the fact that you don't care about Black Lives?"

Suddenly, Shawns delight at Asher's frustration fell away. The question took a moment to process, but when it did, Shawn's levity turned to annoyance, and then anger. "Excuse me? The optics of a grown man punching a fat teenager are bad, but don't think I won't do it."

Asher fell back in his chair. He was wounded by Shawn's comment. "Keep talking. Prove what a hateful monster you are. This office is a safe space, and you dare to fat-shame me?" Asher no longer looked directly at Shawn. His eyes veered off to the side.

Shawn got hold of his senses. The accusation that he didn't care about Black Lives set Shawn off, but he did feel bad about calling the kid fat. Shawn was an adult. He needed to compose himself. He took a deep breath and looked at the ground in shame. He felt bad for insulting a child. "Sorry about that, I should not have said that. I didn't mean to hurt your feelings." Shawn sounded and felt contrite.

However, when Shawn looked up, Asher was dancing in front of his phone's camera again. Asher proceeded to dance for another minute or so. He then picked up his phone, pressed a few buttons, looked back at Shawn, and said, "Sorry, where were we?"

Shawn was clearly annoyed and said in disbelief, "You were telling me how I didn't care about Black Lives."

Asher looked directly at Shawn again. His eyes no longer veered off to the side. "Well, as it turns out, your peers who you won't vote against—they named names. And your name came up a few times. It appears you have told several of your colleagues that you don't think Israel started it."

"What does that have to do with Black Lives?" Shawn was no longer having fun prodding Asher, he no longer felt frustrated at Asher's ignorance, and he no longer felt bad about the way he had talked to Asher. Shawn was just confused and wanted to leave.

"Well, Black Lives posted that they think Israel started it. Therefore, if you don't think Israel started it, how can you support Black Lives?" Asher looked and sounded as though he was about to say "checkmate."

75.0 YEARS BEFORE OPPOSITE DAY DECLARED

Charles Roan

(75 YEARS BEFORE OPPOSITE DAY DECLARED)

The damn ringing in his ears was back. It must have been some kind of sick joke. The last time he had heard the ringing was 25 years ago, when his sister Ruby was killed. He thought that would be the last time. Ruby had been the last one left. There was no more family left to lose after her. Up until now, Charles only thought the ringing came when someone he loved died. But it turns out, they didn't need to die for the ringing to come back. The ringing came back now when someone he loved was leaving.

Charles' wife was telling him that she was leaving with their daughter and moving to Tulsa. At least that's what he thought she was saying, it was hard to tell over the ringing. He knew for sure that she was leaving. He loved her but he wasn't surprised. Charles tried to provide everything for his wife and daughter on their property without the interference of the outside world, and they had luxuries she never could have imagined, but the isolation proved too much.

It was his one rule. He knew that she couldn't live with it, but how could he break it? He had watched as outsiders picked apart his family, member by member. He couldn't just throw back open the doors.

He knew he would still get to see his daughter occasionally, he didn't know how often, that was for the lawyers now. She would never have to deal with a stepmother. Charles was still young enough to remarry, but that would require going to the outside world, and that just wouldn't do. The ringing got louder as he realized that, aside from occasional visits with his daughter, he was all alone.

James Bennet

James Bennet restocked the shelves of the pharmacy where he worked. Restocking shelves had not been his responsibility for years now, but as manager, he wanted to make sure it was done correctly. James thought back to his last 20 years working there. After his family lost their pharmacy during the Tulsa Race Massacre, it felt odd working as an employee at someone else's business, but he needed the money.

James rarely thought directly about his old pharmacy anymore, but when he did, he was left with one simple question: why? It seemed like everyone had a reason or theory on why the violence happened. James didn't believe the clean explanation that this was an isolated incident. He also didn't believe the conspiracy theory that this was the work of real estate interests that wanted to redevelop Greenwood and therefore sparked the violence to clear out the neighborhood. James boiled it down to one issue: the white citizens of Tulsa didn't want to live next to Black people.

It was inconceivable to James that 300 people died because one group of people didn't want to live next to another, but that's what it was. Since then, James became obsessed with the concept of neighbors. He believed it was important to get along with your neighbors, and it was important for neighbors to accept you. He repeated this to his two children over and over. And when his children had children, he told them too.

25.0 YEARS BEFORE OPPOSITE DAY DECLARED

Shawn Bennet

Shawn Bennet was delayed at the airport on his way back to law school. He had come home two weeks earlier because his grandfather James was in his last days, and he stayed for the funeral. Shawn was in a somber mood. It wasn't exactly somber; Shawn was trying to place his feelings. He felt he should have been more somber, but his grandfather was 97. Shawn felt guilty, that's what it was. Shawn felt guilt for not feeling enough internal grief about his grandfather. But that wasn't exactly the feeling either. Maybe he felt guilt about what he always felt guilt about when it came to his grandpa James.

Since Shawn was old enough to understand, he felt guilt about his grandpa James and his grandma Estelle because Shawn was raised in a household that had so much, and his grandparents were poor. The money in his family was from Shawn's mother's side, the Roans. Shawn had always wondered why they couldn't help his grandparents out more, but his father would just throw up his hands and say, "Your grandpa is too proud."

Shawn knew his grandpa was proud. Grandpa James had worked his entire life to save up, but the last years had been particularly difficult for him and Grandma Estelle. Grandma Estelle had fallen victim to a pyramid scheme and lost their entire savings. The con man had wiped out most of the residents in the retirement home.

In the time they had left, Grandpa James never let anyone in the family blame Grandma Estelle for what happened. He would say, "All our neighbors thought it was a good idea, and if it was good enough for them, it was good enough for us. I would have done the same." Grandpa James never relented. Even on his death bed, he talked about the importance of neighbors. By then Shawn had heard it a million times, but still, the fact that he kept it up on his deathbed was impressive.

Now that Shawn had better placed his feelings, he thought back to his delay at the airport. He had enough reading material to study for the flight, but he hadn't anticipated the delay. He decided to watch the TV in the airport rather than burn through his reading. The Liberal News Network was on. He didn't watch much cable news, but he was stuck in the airport, so he didn't have many options.

There was violence in the Middle East. Shawn felt bad in passing, but he had his own problems to think about. The news program showed an interview with one of the leaders of Israel's neighbors. The leader said that Israel's presence in the region was a colonial imposition. Shawn commiserated with that frustration. The leader then said that Israel's presence meant that the Arab world would have to pay for Europe's sins.

Shawn didn't think much of the interview. He dug into his reading material before the flight.

Shawn finished his reading material halfway through his flight. He wished he hadn't started early. Now he just sat bored on the plane with nothing to do. His mind wandered. He thought of the interview he had seen in the airport. For some reason, the phrase "pay for Europe's sins" stuck in his head.

"Paying for Europe's sins" referred to the establishment of Israel after the Holocaust. The leader who was interviewed saw Israel's presence as a burden. Shawn didn't know why this stuck in his head, but it did. Shawn didn't know who started it, but he personally believed that Israel's neighbors didn't want Israel in their neighborhood.

6.0 YEARS AFTER OPPOSITE DAY DECLARED

Shawn Bennet and Asher Mander
(6.0 YEARS AFTER OPPOSITE DAY DECLARED)

Shawn worried that he was about to punch a teenager. He had to keep it together. "Sorry, I'm confused. What does one thing have to do with the other? None of this makes any sense."

Asher now looked as confused as Shawn did. "What doesn't make sense? How can you support Black Lives if you don't think Israel started it? Black Lives said that Israel started it. Therefore, anyone who cares about Black Lives must also think that Israel started it."

Shawn was unconvinced by Asher's logic. "Why? They seem like completely different issues."

Asher looked impassioned and emotional. Shawn could tell he was pissed. "Issues?!?!?!?!?!?!?!?!" Asher yelled. "How can you belittle moral imperatives by referring to them as 'issues?!'" That word is exactly what's wrong with you people."

"You people?" Shawn said half out of reflex and half out of not knowing who Asher was referring to.

Asher got hold of himself, and he looked worried that he went too far. "Sorry, you're right. Persons of your generation," he corrected. "Persons of your generation have political 'issues'. But what you call 'issues', persons of my generation call 'moral imperatives'. We have transcended politics. Politics implies a willingness to remain complicit in the face of evil and hate." Asher continued, "It's simple. We hate hate, and we love likes. The other side loves hate, and hates likes. The

201

only way to stand up to hate is to reject everything that hateful people embrace. The only way to build a society of equality and inclusion is to exclude those who hate."

Shawn's eyes opened wide. He now understood what was happening. "Oh, is this some Opposite Day bullshit? I am really getting sick of this."

But Shawn realized his frustration was futile. The moment he started speaking, Asher started dancing into his phone. Shawn walked out of the office as Asher danced more wildly. Shawn was more disillusioned by the rule of Opposite Day than ever before. He was also surprised by what a good dancer Asher was.

The President (Her/She) and Rex Kellermam
(6.0 YEARS AFTER OPPOSITE DAY DECLARED)

An aide hurried into the Oval Office, carrying an envelope. The President had been waiting for this notice and gave instructions to let her know as soon as it arrived.

"Sorry to interrupt Ma'am, but we have just received word back from the Governor of Tennessee. He has requested you make a disaster declaration to help with the recovery from Hurricane Leslie."

Much like Hurricane Lisa, which had hit the Tennessee Valley four years earlier, Hurricane Leslie uncharacteristically gained strength as it made its way over land. The predominantly white male meteorologists said that hurricane Lisa was anomalous and unlikely to happen again, but the hurricane's voice had only grown stronger over the last four years and was ready to break through the recently repaired glass ceiling. The Tennessee Valley had only recently started recovering from hurricane Lisa when Hurricane Leslie hit, because initial recovery efforts from Lisa were stymied due to public backlash against the selfish nature of the region's inhabitants.

The President had prepared for this letter to arrive. She called over Rex Kellermam, her most trusted and loyal advisor, from where he was perched near the door surveying the room, to help plan a response.

The President felt distraught at the destruction and human suffering caused by the meteorologists who were too myopic to fully hear and appreciate Hurricane Leslie's voice. No matter how nasty and hurtful the residents of the Tennessee Valley had been, The President wanted nothing more than to send her thoughts and prayers to those who were impacted. But she remembered Rex's advice to "act more presidential".

Since Rex had given her that advice, she had followed it to the letter. She changed the way she spoke to better fit her ideal vision of the office and disallowed the use of all phones in the conduct of presidential business.

The President snapped into action with instructions for Rex. "With haste, draft a letter to FEMA declaring a disaster, and alert the Governor that his pecuniary needs should not be for wanting within a fortnight."

Rex wanted to speak up, but he just couldn't. It wasn't his place. At least, he didn't think it was his place. But of all the mismanagement he had seen in the last year and a half of her presidency, this one had the potential to do the most damage. "Madam President." Rex had to keep from swallowing his words. "Wouldn't the funds get there faster if we just called FEMA this one time?"

The President looked at Rex with a ravenous longing in her eyes. Did he mean what he just said? How she longed for her phone again! To share her likes, to send her thoughts and her prayers, to lend moral support to the right causes, and to condemn those online who showed a lack of morality. But she had come too far to regress now.

The President had to do what was right for the country. She brushed aside her longing for her phone and replied, "Rex, as you know, the loss of my phone has filled me with pangs of sadness which shake me at night too deeply for my own repose. While using my phone again would agitate my spirits in the most agreeable fashion, I should think such an action too imprudent at the present."

Shawn Bennet

When Shawn got to the Chamber the next morning, every representative from both parties was there. Shawn knew that all Liberals were instructed by leadership to attend, but he wasn't sure why the Conservatives showed up in such force.

Shawn wasn't sure which way the Conservatives would vote. They hated the far left of the party more than they hated Frank and the rest of The Walking Dead. It didn't matter. Geraldine Mander and leadership had the votes. Shawn thought about the math. Of the 432 members, 167 were Conservative and 275 were Liberal. Assuming Shawn and the other members of The Walking Dead voted against stripping their committee assignments, they still needed to convert 101 votes.

Shawn looked over at Frank, who looked calm. Shawn figured Frank had resigned himself to his fate. When Conservative leadership walked by, Shawn saw Frank nod his head, and believed they nodded back at Frank. Shawn thought nothing of it. Many of the most senior members of the House Conservatives were frequent attendees at Frank's predictions on the jobs report. They made a lot of money off those meetings. Maybe Frank had convinced them to vote with him. But even that wouldn't make much of a difference—101 votes were still a lot of votes to make up.

While they waited for the vote, Shawn heard rumblings through the Chamber. Shawn was so focused on the vote that he forgot it was also a jobs report Friday. He didn't normally get involved in Frank's market predictions, but he knew what they were this month. Frank needed all the help he could get.

Shawn knew that Frank had told everyone in his meeting to buy the market before the jobs report. As Shawn understood it, the report was supposed to be terrible. The country was supposed to lose at least 350k jobs. This was good for the stock market, because even though it was bad for the economy, it meant that the Fed would not raise interest rates. If they kept interest rates low, it would be good for business, because credit would be readily available for companies to continue taking on debt to buy back stock. Frank explained this to Shawn upwards of 15 times, but Shawn didn't fully understand it.

Shawn looked through the jobs report. The country added 2.5 million jobs! The unemployment rate went from 4 percent all the way to 2.5 percent! This meant the economy was resoundingly strong. Using the logic that Frank laid out, Shawn realized this was bad for the stock market. The underlying economy was too strong, which was bad for business because it meant the Fed would raise rates. Moreover, this was bad for Frank's prediction on the market. Anyone who had bought ahead of this report was likely to lose a lot of money. Shawn realized that Frank would not get much help today from anyone who bought the market on his recommendation.

Shawn looked around the room after he read through the jobs report. He saw a scene of chaos and anger. Members of Congress were incensed when they saw how many jobs the US economy had added. One thing Shawn saw in the report was that job creation was most significant in the Black community. U.S. Black unemployment fell from 7 percent to 4 percent. While this was still higher than unemployment levels in the overall economy, it was an improvement. Shawn looked over to the head of the National Black Caucus to nod his approval, but saw the head of the National Black Caucus was looking at the job creation and having a panic attack about the havoc in the stock market it would cause.

Shawn noticed that while there was panic on the Liberal side of the floor, there was calm over on the Conservative side. Shawn thought back to the exchange between Frank and the Conservative leadership and realized what Frank had done. Knowing what this jobs number would be, Frank had secured the Conservative vote. But they would still have to make up 101 votes.

The House was called to order right as the stock market opened for the trading day. But just as soon as the market opened, the market closed. The economy was strong, the market fell 7 percent. This tripped the first of three market circuit breakers. If the market falls 7 percent, a circuit breaker goes into effect closing the market for 15 minutes. When the market opens back up, if it continues to fall, to down 13 percent, a second circuit breaker is tripped, closing the market for another 15 minutes. If the market continues to fall, to down 20 percent, the market is closed for the day.

Speaker Mander began the roll call vote just as the market reopened from its first circuit breaker. Under the rules of a roll call vote, each member is called on to say "aye" or "no" on a proposal. The first member who voted was a Conservative who voted "no." With that, Shawn confirmed that Frank had secured the Conservative vote. As the vote began, some members who took Frank's recommendation to buy the market left the Chamber. They needed to sell their stock before they lost more. Shawn counted 20 members who left the floor. If they did not come back, they would still need to close the gap on 81 votes.

Unemployment was low, the market fell another 5 percent. The market was now down 13 percent, which tripped the second circuit breaker, closing the stock market for another 15 minutes. Before Shawn voted, a few Conservative and Liberal members voted along party lines. Voting was ordered alphabetically, so Shawn was one of the first to vote. He stood up to vote. He voted, "no." There was absolute silence. If anyone were to break with the party, he was the most likely person, but no one expected him to follow through with it.

The Chamber seemed shell-shocked. Speaker Mander was stone-faced and emotionless. Shawn could tell she was pissed.

The vote continued. Members voted along party lines. The market was still closed for the second circuit breaker. Frank and Shawn still needed to convert 81 votes. Then, Ellen Coleman, a Liberal representative from Michigan, stood up to vote. She voted "no." The Chamber was stunned. Ellen Coleman was a third-term representative. She was not a member of The Walking Dead. She was expected to vote along party lines. While HUAC only brought up members of The Walking Dead on charges, there were rumblings that Ellen would be accused of thoughtless crime in the next round of hearings. Ellen's adult son was a police officer. In an interview that had since resurfaced, Ellen mentioned that she worried about his safety when he was on duty. Her concern for his life was deemed problematic.

The chamber was stunned. Geraldine Mander looked stone-faced and emotionless. Shawn could tell she was pissed. While Shawn's defection was possible but not fully expected, Ellen's defection was a surprise. Of the next 10 Liberals to vote, there were three more defections. The flood gates were open.

A Liberal member objected, demanding that a quorum was not present. This was a procedural ploy to stop the bleeding. The vote would start from the beginning and be taken electronically. This would require approval by one-fifth of the members present. It also required more time. The market was about to reopen after the second circuit breaker. If the market fell another 7 percent, it would close for the day. This could be the last opportunity of the day for members who had not already sold stock to do so. As the market's reopening approached, members started to trickle out. Soon, the trickle became a flood. Shawn counted 30 members who left the chamber. That meant they needed to convert 26 more votes from the 40 Liberals left to vote.

Geraldine Mander (She/Her)
(6.0 YEARS AFTER OPPOSITE DAY DECLARED)

It wasn't a matter of winning or losing the vote. Geraldine knew she would win. She had enough tricks up her sleeve. She needed to maintain her supermajority. If she didn't, she would lose it forever.

There was so much left to be done. So much inequality in society to address. Geraldine knew she needed to fix the world, not for herself, but for Asher and his generation. She knew that if she didn't, Asher would tell his children and his children's children that she was a monster. Thoughtless crime didn't only apply to actions of the past. Future generations would have thoughtless crime, and Geraldine knew they would judge her. She didn't know what she would be judged for, so she made sure to cover all her bases.

She looked at Frank and Shawn. They were smiling. Why were they smiling? They couldn't possibly think they would win. Supermajority or not, she would still win the vote, and Frank and the rest of those hoodlums would be stripped of their committee seats.

Geraldine watched the 30 members leave the chamber. She wasn't angry with them. She would bury them, but she wasn't angry. Why did everyone assume she was always angry? She didn't like burying bodies; it was unpleasant business. She felt pity for the members leaving the room. Geraldine was losing money in the stock markets as well, but she had the decency to have enough money so that one day's losses would not matter.

As she looked at the peons scrambling out of the Chamber attempting to save their money, Geraldine realized the problem. The problem was that the legislators in her party weren't rich enough to enact real change. Only representatives with money to burn had the will to enact meaningful change.

Patricia Ocampo Santos (She/Her)
(6.0 YEARS AFTER OPPOSITE DAY DECLARED)

Those greedy fucks. As Patricia looked at the fat cats rushing out of the chamber attempting to save their money, she realized the problem. The problem with the party was that everyone was too wealthy. How could they fix income inequality when her "peers" were the ones whose wealth needed to be redistributed? Only those who wanted to burn money had the will to enact meaningful change.

Patricia looked at Geraldine Mander. She saw that Geraldine was also watching these pigs scramble to save their place at the trough. Geraldine looked stone-faced and emotionless. Patricia could tell she was pissed. Patricia made sure to take note of everyone who left the Chamber. They would be next in front of the committee. There would be consequences. She knew Geraldine wanted the role of burying the bodies, but this wasn't her battle. Patricia wanted to be the one to take care of it.

Speaker Mander called for a recess before the electronic vote started. Patricia looked at her phone. She had several missed calls and texts from Rory. She left the chamber to call him. "We are in the middle of a vote. I can't talk for long." Patricia skipped all formalities.

Rory was calling from the hospital. After the hearings the night before, his condition got worse. The doctors did not sound optimistic. They were doing their best to manage his pain, but his body was shutting down.

211

Rory also skipped any form of greeting. He was too worried about what he was seeing. "This is too close. It's a big problem."

Patricia thought Rory was over-reacting. "Speaker Mander is waiting for everyone to get back into the Chamber. There is no chance they'll win. And trust me, when this is over, we will go after everyone who voted against us, and everyone who left the chamber."

"They don't need to win. They need to make you look weak. If you look weak, there will be no committee," Rory explained.

"I don't think one vote will have that sort of impact." Patricia initially tried to brush off Rory's concern, but his point was sinking in. "They are too afraid to turn on me. Even my critics call me a 'demigod'."

"I think you're hearing that word wrong," Rory gently corrected. "But you're not untouchable. You need to win big or there will be no committee to hold the traitors accountable. Trust me."

"Don't be so dramatic." Patricia stopped herself from calling Rory a baby out loud or in her head. She paused for a moment to recognize her personal growth.

Rory's voice trembled as he changed the subject. "Honey, the doctors think I'm dying. I'm scared."

"You really shouldn't talk like that," Patricia responded, not in a comforting but corrective tone. "The dead are an underrepresented group in society. Your fear is highly offensive to them," Patricia further explained.

Rory choked back his concern. He knew that Patricia was right. "Thank you for this teachable moment. I wouldn't have traded our time together for anything."

"Of course. Without teachable moments, what would be the point?" As Patricia hung up the phone, she felt a sense of companionship that could only be achieved by fully connecting with another person during a teachable moment.

Frank Vultaggio

(6.0 YEARS AFTER OPPOSITE DAY DECLARED)

Frank looked at the dummies running out of the Chamber. Fish in a barrel. He looked at his watch. He wanted the vote to start so they could get this over with. This was fun for a bit, but he was bored now. When the market opened from the second circuit breaker, Frank used his phone to put in orders to buy stocks. He knew it was against the rules to use his phone on the floor, but what were they gonna do, kick him out? Anyways, it's like his grandmother always told him, *Fuck 'em if they can't take a joke.*

Frank's time in Washington had been very profitable. He couldn't wait to get home. Not only did he have the money he'd made, he'd also be a folk hero back home after telling POS to "blow it out her ass". He would never have to pay for a drink again.

Frank then thought back to the vote and got worried. He didn't expect Shawn to outright vote "no". He had told Shawn it would be OK if Shawn voted against him. *Guy's got balls, I'll give him that*, he thought to himself. But Frank was definitely not expecting the large-scale defection in the Liberal Party. He needed the members who left the chamber to come back and vote. He was nervous he would actually win this thing. Then he would be stuck here. That would suck so hard.

Shawn Bennet

hawn looked over at Frank, who kept checking his phone. Shawn could tell Frank was nervous about the vote, so he put his hand on Frank's shoulder to show his support. He felt bad for Frank. He knew this was traumatic for him.

The market opened after the 15-minute pause for the second circuit breaker. Shawn thought about the legislators who were off the floor trading stocks. He felt bad, but he didn't care if they lost money; he wished they would stay out there trading and not come back onto the floor and vote. If only they would stay out there, Frank could win this.

When the stock market opened again, it fell another 2 percent, to down 15 percent. Shawn was worried—if the market continued to fall like this, it would be down 20 percent in no time and would close for the day. If it closed, the legislators who had left the room would have nothing to trade and would come back and vote.

But the market stabilized at down 15 percent for a few minutes. Then it began to climb. In no time, it recovered 5 percent and was down 10 percent on the day.

When the market stabilized at down 10 percent, Speaker Mander called the session back into order, and the electronic vote began. After a few minutes, the legislators who had left the floor filed back in. With each legislator who came back, Shawn felt more despair. Soon all 50 legislators were back.

As he watched the tally of electronic votes, Shawn noticed something strange. One of the two Liberal members who had voted before Shawn in the roll call vote changed her vote. She now voted "no." But Shawn didn't get his hopes up. The 50 members were all back now, and Frank couldn't win unless he converted 25 of them. But Frank had no chance of converting them. He just cost them all a lot of money. How could he expect to get their votes now?

Patricia Ocampo Santos (Her/She)
(6.0 YEARS AFTER OPPOSITE DAY DECLARED)

Patricia stood outside the door of the Chamber. The only way to keep her supermajority was to convince these animals who had left the floor to vote with her. But how could she reach them? They were greedy by nature. She had nothing in common with them. Whenever Patricia didn't know what to do, she could always count on the wise words she had said in previous conversations to guide her through her troubles.

She thought back to her conversation a few minutes before with Rory. When Rory recklessly slandered the underrepresented and often-oppressed class of persons who were deceased, Patricia did not chastise him. She used it as a teachable moment, and he appreciated it. Why was this any different?

As each of the 50 members who had left the floor slunk back in, Patricia greeted them at the door with her message of tolerance and understanding. "It's not your fault your greed got the best of you. Now that you have lost all your money, you see how capitalism isn't the answer. Thank you for your continued support, and I look forward to attacking thoughtless crime in all its forms."

Geraldine Mander (She/Her)

(6.0 YEARS AFTER OPPOSITE DAY DECLARED)

Geraldine stood at the podium and watched the 50 members return to their seats. She needed to keep her supermajority and couldn't afford any more defections. As much as she hated it, she would have to let these poor slobs off the hook for leaving. Luckily, she was a master of non-verbal communication. She would use one of her world-famous looks to tell them that all was forgiven.

Shawn Bennet

(6.0 YEARS AFTER OPPOSITE DAY DECLARED)

Shawn looked at Speaker Mander as she watched the 50 members come back onto the floor. She looked stone-faced and emotionless. He could tell she was pissed.

He watched the vote. It felt like forever. With each vote against them, he thought this would be easier if it was just a blow-out, because they wouldn't get their hopes up. Each vote for them was euphoric. They were pulling off a coup.

When the 50 members who came back from trading stocks finished voting, 24 of them had voted "no". It was incredible; that conversion rate was nearly twice the rate they had for the overall party. It was a miracle, or there must have been some other outside forces working in their favor. But while the vote said they were tied at 217-217, they only got 24 of the 25 votes they needed. Shawn realized that meant there was still one vote left. Speaker Mander hadn't voted yet. Shawn's heart broke for Frank. They had come so close and now all was lost.

Geraldine Mander

(6.0 YEARS AFTER OPPOSITE DAY DECLARED)

Geraldine Mander stood at her podium. She couldn't believe it came down to this, but she had to vote. She assumed they would have enough of a majority that she wouldn't need to. Speakers only voted when the vote was close. She thought about Asher. She lost the supermajority. She was doomed. Her name would live in infamy, cursed through the generations. What thoughtless crimes would she be accused of in the future? She shuddered. Everything she did from here was meaningless. No matter what good she achieved, it wouldn't be enough. Her future thoughtless crime would wipe it all away.

But what if she didn't allow that to happen? She was a voting member of Congress. She could use her vote to fight the establishment of thoughtless crime. If she fought hard enough, maybe she would be successful. The only way to stop Asher from dragging her name through the mud was to vote against HUAC.

Frank Vultaggio

(6.0 YEARS AFTER OPPOSITE DAY DECLARED)

Frank watched as Geraldine Mander prepared to vote. She was looking directly at him. Frank had enough cousins who had been in court to know that if a jury came back from deliberating and looked directly at the defendant, they were likely to acquit. He had a terrible feeling that Geraldine was about to vote "no". Ugh! He couldn't deal with this anymore. He just wanted to go home. Frank needed to do something to stop her. Luckily, he was a master of non-verbal communication. Frank looked directly at Geraldine and proceeded to mouth the filthiest, most vile phrase he could think of.

Shawn Bennet

Shawn felt so bad for Frank. One vote. They came so close, and they lost by one vote. Ughhhhh. Shawn wanted to scream. He put his hand on Frank's shoulder as Frank sat silently. His sadness was palpable.

Eventually, Shawn got up to leave. As he did, he saw the 58 Liberal members who broke ranks to vote with him all getting up simultaneously. He left the Chamber, and they followed him. He walked out of the Capitol Building; they continued to follow. Shawn got on the train to head to his apartment. They got on the train as well. Shawn was almost certain they were following him at this point, but he wanted to make sure. At the first stop, he exited the train car and moved to the next train car. They got off the train car and got onto the next train car. Shawn got off the train at his stop. They followed him off the train. When they got to the street, Shawn stopped, turned around, and asked loudly, "Why are you following me?"

Ellen Coleman, the representative from Michigan, who was the first to defect after Shawn, stepped forward. "Where else are we supposed to go?" she asked.

"What do you mean? Why are you following me?" Shawn thought it was odd that he was always confused, and others seemed to think their behavior was normal. Shawn was pretty sure he didn't miss any days of orientation, but what other explanation could there be? What was wrong with everyone?

"We voted with you. Now we are awaiting further instruction on how to vote going forward," Ellen explained.

Shawn looked perplexed, "Why would you ask me? I've been here for a year. I barely know where the bathrooms are. Why should I tell you how to vote?"

"Well, are we Liberal? Are we Conservative?" Ellen asked. She looked as though she were waiting for Shawn to unburden her with a simple answer.

"Why not just vote what you feel?" Shawn asked.

Ellen looked relieved. "So, we are Liberal?" she half asked.

Cheers arose from the 58 representatives who followed Shawn.

"No. You know … I mean, vote what you think," Shawn immediately corrected himself.

Ellen continued to look relieved. "Oh, so we are Conservative?"

Cheers arose from the 58 representatives who followed Shawn.

"No," Shawn corrected himself again. "I mean vote how you want to vote on each individual topic. Treat each vote like a choice. Sometimes you will vote Liberal, and sometimes you will vote Conservative."

"Oh. OK. I get it. So how will you let us know when to vote Liberal or Conservative?" Ellen had a hopeful tone as her voice crescendoed through her question.

Shawn shook his head, both indicating *no* and showing exasperation. "No, it's whatever you decide."

"Oh, I get it." Ellen responded before she winked at Shawn.

Shawn walked away from the group on the street. He wasn't fully sure they understood his point, but he had had enough for the day. No one else seemed to be bothered by this Opposite Day nonsense. He felt that he was the only one in a constant state of confusion. Shawn walked the remainder of the way home feeling exhausted and alone, isolated from others by his confusion. He had never expected to win the vote, but coming so close and losing had drained him of his hope.

When Shawn got home, he had all but given up. He contemplated making arrangements to head back to Tulsa when he received a message from The President's office saying she wanted to meet with him in the morning.

The Committee to Unify National Tories
(6.0 YEARS AFTER OPPOSITE DAY DECLARED)

Billie and Wilma D. watched the Liberal's ignominious victory with great interest. Now that there was dissent within the Liberal ranks, it was time for Billie and Wilma D. to make their move. They would not just gain back the ground they had lost in the last few years; they would make up for lost time.

Billie and Wilma D. could not take credit for this strategy, that was the algorithm of the political pendulum they detected. When one party gained power and the other party was temporarily marginalized, the party in power would satiate the needs of their most far-reaching desires first. Then, when public appetite grew weary of the extremity of changes that were made, more moderate measures would be taken up by the party in control. But by then, it was too late to get those changes passed, and the political pendulum would swing the other way, bringing the other party to power, to champion the extremities of their party's beliefs.

Billie and Wilma sensed that they were at the dawning of their political spring and would therefore need to bring forward their plans. The next step would be to have their rising star meet with Conservative Party leadership, Wesley Johnston. However, Billie and Wilma would also attend the meeting with Wesley. Even though Jeffery Tripp Perez ranked very high on most of the indicative variables of a rising star, from impressionability to non-threatening good looks, he was still an unintentional loose cannon.

The President (Her/She),
Shawn Bennet, and Rex Kellermam
(6.0 Years after Opposite Day Declared)

"**C**ongressman Bennet, I bid you come in." The President sounded welcoming when Shawn appeared at the Oval Office for their meeting.

Shawn sat across from the President. "Thank you for meeting with me Madam President."

It made The President so sad to see the fighting in Congress, but she knew Shawn did what was right. "It was with great trepidation that I watched your recent struggle, but your stand is deserving of the most sincere approbation, lest the halls of Congress have been overtaken with the malignant air of calumny."

Shawn took a moment to think about what The President just said. Like the rest of the country, he was thoroughly impressed by her transformation but utterly confused when she spoke. "Thank you, but unfortunately we lost." Shawn still felt deflated that the other members of The Walking Dead, especially Frank, had been so unceremoniously stripped of their committee assignments.

The President's thoughts and prayers went out to the members of The Walking Dead, but she knew that even though Shawn lost the vote, he had been so brave, and she was in awe of his courage. "While victory proved elusive, once the transient circumstances of the vote have faded, your steadfastness will warrant the notice of posterity."

"Thank you?" Shawn didn't mean to phrase it as a question, but he rushed out his response because he didn't want The President to think he was being rude if she had in fact complimented him.

Shawn looked to Rex Kellermam, the President's most trusted and loyal advisor, hoping for a clue to help him keep up with what The President was saying. Shawn figured if anyone knew, it would be Rex. However, Rex was all the way over at the entrance of the office, standing stoically as though he were surveying the room.

The President saw Shawn look over at Rex and realized it would be best for Rex to more actively take part in the meeting. "Rex, come forth and join the Congressman and me."

Shawn noticed Rex's face turn from blank stare to a cautionary raise of his eyebrows as he timidly looked over at the Secret Service agents posted at other points in the room, as if to ask permission to approach Shawn and The President.

As Rex cautiously approached, The President refocused on the business of the meeting. Her presidency was supposed to be about hating hate, and the increased fighting in the country made her so, so sad. She wanted to pass laws to end hatred. Shawn's bill to end fraud against senior citizens seemed perfect. Especially because the Former President, who she was so blessed to have known, had fallen victim to these heartless schemes.

"With each passing day, we slip further into a state of perpetual internal acrimony. Should we respond with reticence, the factional enmity that has gripped our nation threatens to tear us asunder. I have endeavored to find an issue that was both agreeable to the spirits of the largest number of citizens, as well as an expedient remedy to a scourge that has plagued our land and is close to my heart. As you are certainly aware, the Former President fell victim to several of these villains who prey on the elderly. For too long have these scoundrels committed inequity with impunity. Your efforts to protect senior citizens from fraud is that such issue for which I have searched, and I wish to play a most conspicuous role in this enterprise."

Shawn had to think for a minute. He wasn't sure how to respond or what exactly The President had said. The more he thought about it, the more it sounded like she wanted to help him with his legislation. That would be a dream come true. Shawn looked over at Rex to see if there was a clue on Rex's face or from his body language that could confirm The President's intent, but Rex looked to be only focused on surveying the room.

Shawn couldn't contain himself. "You mean to tell me you would like to help with my bill to protect senior citizens from fraud?"

The President knowingly smiled at Rex in a way that made Shawn feel as though he asked a stupid question. "I fear that Congress has grown too capricious in its whims to take on a matter of this import. A National Declaration of Emergency should serve as a breastwork for our cause until a more suitable permanent accommodation can be made."

The President then looked again at Rex, "What say you?"

Rex took a break from surveying the room to address The President. "At the moment there are no visible or known threats to your person."

Shawn thought that was an odd response, but he had become numb to a lot weirder nonsense in the last few months.

The President then replied to Rex, "Wonderful, contact the Justice Department to make the needed arrangements."

Rex nodded his understanding. "I will get started on a letter right away."

The President then smiled at Shawn in a manner that made Shawn sense that Rex had made a silly error. The President then turned from Shawn to look at Rex. "In this matter, I believe a call to be more expeditious to our ends than a letter."

Jeffery Tripp Perez and
The Committee to Unify National Tories
(6.0 Years after Opposite Day Declared)

Wesley Johnston would have been a veteran of the Korean War, but he was disqualified from service because General MacArthur wanted to make it a fair fight. Had he served in the Army, he would have been a career military man, working his way up to Major and then retiring. Wesley could have made it all the way up to General, but in order to do that, he would have had to be a Colonel. That is why he would have retired at Major.

Major was a solid rank, a man's title. Colonel was for sissies, with all its deceptive letters sounding like other letters. Had the army been willing to change the spelling to Kurnel or even Cournel, Wesley would have been willing to stay in his hypothetical military career. He would have preferred the spelling with the "K" though. "C" was one of those deceptive letters. With a "K," you always knew what you were getting, and when it failed to make its normal sound, it was silent, like a good soldier should be. That's why nothing bad ever started with the letter "K".

"C", on the other hand, could sometimes make the sound of an "S". Wesley remembered a time in this country when "C's" were "C's" and "S's" were "S's." Now a "C" could be an "S" if it wanted to. What was next, could a "C" be an "R"? That's what would happen if the Liberals had their way.

228

Billie and Wilma D. traveled with Jeffery Tripp Perez to Branson, Missouri to meet with Wesley Johnston. They were able to schedule a meeting for Jeffery to meet Wesley, but Wesley was busy, so they had to meet while Wesley was between meetings. They sat outside Wesley's room until the nurse let them in.

When they entered the room, Wesley sat on a reclining chair in front of a TV, wrapping up his previous meeting. On the TV was the Conservative Conservative News Network. While before the last election there had been only two news networks, Conservative Conservative viewers had become disgusted with the Liberal bias of the Conservative News Network and demanded the creation of the Conservative Conservative News Network.

When Jeffery, Billie D., and Wilma D. walked into the room, the TV was blasting, and a reporter on the Conservative Conservative News Network was completing a segment on how the Woke Mafia was doing their best to play victim again. This time, the Woke Mafia demanded federal charges be brought against a Conservative congressman accused of statutory rape, because the "victim" had been transported over state lines.

When the segment was over, the newscast went to commercial break. As soon as the commercials started, Wesley lifted a very large remote control from the armrest of his reclining chair. The remote control was double the size of most other TV remotes that Jeffery had seen, but this remote had fewer buttons, which were also much larger than normal.

Wesley pressed mute on the remote and looked over at Billie and Wilma D. before acknowledging Jeffery. "This new guy Jacobs that the Conservative Conservative network just hired away from the Conservative network is the real deal. He just gets it."

Billie and Wilma knew that Wesley was spot on. He had his hand on the pulse of the Conservative Party. Jacobs' defection from the Conservative News Network to the Conservative Conservative News

Network was the epitome of the issue with both the Conservative News Network and the less committed members of the Conservative Party. They were not evolving with the party.

Billie D. replied to Wesley, "We concur with your assessment."

Jeffery then stepped forward, spat on his hand, and stretched his arm out to shake hands with Wesley. "Major Johnston, it is an honor to meet you. Thank you for your hypothetical service."

Wesley looked at the outstretched hand with a giant ball of phlegm in the center of Jeffery's palm in absolute disgust. He then looked over to Billie and Wilma D.

Billie and Wilma D. knew this was a disastrous scenario. How could Jeffery make such a disgusting faux pas? Billie and Wilma D. did their best to make an expression on their faces they had seen others make, called cringing.

Wesley, still not directly acknowledging Jeffery's presence, scoffed at Billie and Wilma D. "I thought you said your rising star was a Conservative? Seems like a weak-kneed Liberal to me."

Jeffery, realizing his blunder, pulled back his hand quickly, making a point of not hiding his embarrassment. As Jeffery pulled back his hand, he simultaneously opened his mouth. When Wesley saw Jeffery open his mouth, Wesley slowly and loudly pulled back his head collecting mucus from his throat. Wesley then spat into Jeffery's open mouth. Once Jeffery swallowed, he proceeded to reciprocate into Wesley's now open mouth.

After Wesley and Jeffery spat into each other's mouths, they looked at each other and simultaneously said, "Not in a gay way."

Billie and Wilma D. looked on the second greeting attempt knowing Jeffery had salvaged the introduction.

Wesley, now addressing Jeffery directly, said, "Your generation is terrible. My generation are all better people than you."

Jeffery nodded his head in earnest disappointment. "I know."

Wesley made a proud grin, and then, addressing Billie and Wilma D. said, "I like this guy. He gets it." Wesley then looked back over at Jeffery and said, "I have to go to my next meeting. Can you stick around? I should be done in about 15 minutes."

Jeffery felt relieved that he was able to salvage his meeting. He knew that now was the time for him to press his luck. "Major Johnston, I don't mean to be too forward, but I believe there is a lot I could learn from sitting in on your meeting. Would you mind if I joined you?"

Wesley couldn't contain an ear-to-ear smile. "By all means." Wesley then lifted the large remote from his armrest and pressed unmute as the Conservative Conservative newscast came back from commercial break. He sat in his recliner as Jeffery stood at his side, both watching the upcoming segment.

Owen Cosgrove
(6.0 YEARS AFTER OPPOSITE DAY DECLARED)

Owen Cosgrove stumbled exhaustedly into his editor's office. Ever since Jacobs defected to the Conservative Conservative News Network, the editor had been running Owen and the rest of the reporters at the Conservative News Network ragged.

When Owen came into the editor's office, the editor took little notice of or didn't care about Owen's condition. The editor barked, "What you got for me?"

Owen shrugged. "Not a whole lot I can confirm just yet."

"Confirm!" the editor said in a mocking tone. Owen knew he was in for it, of all the words that triggered the editor, none set him off like the word "confirm."

"While you are out '*confirming*' your precious stories," the editor continued, making sure to put extra emphasis on the word confirm, "we are getting our lunch eaten."

Owen was exhausted. He and the rest of the newsroom had been working breathlessly to cover for the loss of just one reporter, after Jacobs left to join the Conservative Conservative Network. The sheer volume of stories that Jacobs churned out was incredible. Owen had no idea how Jacobs did it.

The editor wasn't done with Owen. "Ever since Jacobs left, all I hear are words like 'confirm' or 'check' or 'corroborate'. When Jacobs was here, I never heard those words."

Owen was starting to understand how Jacobs churned out so many stories. Owen began to explain what he had been working on. "Boss, I've been in contact with …" but before he could finish, the editor cut him off.

"What have you even been working on, if anything?" the editor asked, not acknowledging that Owen had been speaking.

Owen started from the beginning. "Boss, I've been in contact with my source in the White House and … "

The editor rolled his eyes. "Ugh, what is Chandra saying now, and how much time are you asking for?"

Owen continued, "Boss, have you ever wondered who this Rex Kellermam is? He is the President's most trusted and influential advisor, and yet no one has heard of him. But my source at the White House says that Rex Kellermam isn't even his real name."

The editor fell back in his chair, frantically waving his arms. "You mean he could be a plant from the Woke Mafia?" the editor half asked, and half stated.

Owen tried to walk the editor back before he got too excited. "I'm not sure about that. It all seems odd, but I can't be sure yet that it's anything nefarious."

The editor sat forward in his chair, grabbed the front of his desk with his hands, and proceeded to bang his head full force onto the desktop two times. Owen had seen the editor react with a full range of emotions in the past: excitement, anger, fear. But never anything like this.

Owen knew he was in the editor's doghouse ever since his last big story failed to expose the Woke Mafia, even if it did unearth a national security breach that led to the downfall of The Former President.

The editor picked his head up from the desk. His nose was bloodied and clearly broken. "Owen, are you telling me that this Rex Kellermam could be a plant from the Woke Mafia, infiltrating the office of the executive?"

Owen had never heard the editor use his first name before. He knew this was serious. "I mean, I could look into a connection, but there is nothing that indicates that right now."

The editor shuddered. He again grabbed the front of his desk with his hands and proceeded to plow his face full force into his desk. But this time, he did not stop after the second slam. He continued a third and fourth time.

Finally, Owen couldn't take it anymore. "Alright, alright, it sounds like there is a connection. I will find one."

The editor looked up at Owen with a thankful and delirious smile. "Thank you. Find what you can. Either way, we run it this evening." Owen could see that along with a broken nose, the editor was bleeding from the mouth and missing several teeth.

Jeffery Tripp Perez and Wesley Johnston
(6.0 YEARS AFTER OPPOSITE DAY DECLARED)

Jeffery Tripp Perez sat in on Wesley Johnston's meetings all day. One meeting blended into the next, and Jeffery learned more and more. But more importantly, Jeffery and Wesley saw that the other thought as he thought, and believed in what he believed in.

As Jacobs laid out the issues in each segment, Jeffery and Wesley got angry at the same reports of Liberal treachery, scared by the same facts about immigration, and laughed at the same Liberal missteps as they were reported throughout the day.

At first, Billie and Wilma D. stayed in the room, but they left at some point, and Jeffery and Wesley stayed for hours, taking meeting after meeting, comparing notes and takeaways between each segment. They were in perfect agreement.

As the day drew to a close, Wesley turned towards Jeffery. "You know, it's rare that someone of your generation gets it. A lot of them say they do, but they don't."

Jeffery looked at Wesley. He had never received this sort of confidence from another person. Not from Billie and Wilma D., nor from his own family. "Thank you for your confidence, Major Johnston."

Wesley knew they had just met, but he felt a bond with Jeffery. "Please, no need to be so formal. You can just call me Major Wesley."

Jeffery blushed. "OK, Major Wesley." Jeffery knew he had permission, but it felt odd to address someone of such gravitas in such an informal way.

Wesley then turned graver. "You know, Jeffery, me and my generation won't be around for much longer."

"Don't say that. What will we do?" Jeffery begged.

Wesley looked at peace. "Until I met you, I wasn't sure. My generation has pondered this question for a long time now. How will the world get along without us? That is why we have stuck around for so long. Not for us, but because we knew that the generations behind us weren't ready to take the reins of the world. But now that we have met, I know that our society will be in good hands."

For once, Jeffery found something that he cared about more than how his star was rising. "Don't leave us. You can't."

Wesley gave Jeffery a strange look. "Yeah, I mean, I'm not dying right now. I'll still be around for a while, but I just mean, when me and my generation do decide to go."

Jeffery at first felt relieved, but then also felt a pang of impatience. Now that the immediate threat to Wesley and his generation was removed, the elevation of Jeffery's star moved back to the forefront of his mind. Jeffery worried that his star would never reach its proper zenith if Wesley and his generation continued on.

"Well, whenever you do decide to go, just know that the party will be in capable hands." Jeffery tried to sound as engaged as before, but his impatience for Wesley's generation to move out of the way started to gnaw at him.

Wesley did not pick up on any change from Jeffery. "Just remember, you won't only be the head of the party, you will be the only thing protecting the country from Liberals trampling on our individual rights. Our personal freedoms are under constant attack from Liberals. You heard what Jacobs said. Liberals attack our personal freedoms with their right to gay marriage, their right to abortion, and especially their right for the undocumented to enter this country."

Jeffery nodded his agreement and added, "Don't forget what Jacobs said about division. All these Liberals want to do is divide, divide, divide. They would rather see Conservatives fail than win themselves. It's crazy. I just can't wait to see Liberals fail, even if it means they burn down half the country. I just want to see the look on their faces."

Wesley nodded his agreement, picked up the remote, and pressed unmute so that he and Jeffery could take one last meeting together.

Rex Kellermam

Rex Kellermam surveyed the road for threats as he drove home from work. Of course there were no threats, and after a few moments, he tried to shake it off. It was hard to reduce his vigilance after a shift spent looking for all possible sources of bodily harm.

Rex saw that his wife was calling but decided he would pretend he didn't see the call. He was only a few minutes away from home and would see her then. Rex needed time to relax and think, and he wouldn't have any answers to the questions she would ask about his job. He had the same unanswered questions.

Rex went through the list of anticipated questions his wife would ask when he got home as well as the only answer he had to each question.

Have you figured out what's going on at work? I don't know.

Are you still a member of the Secret Service or are you an advisor to The President? I don't know.

Is there someone you can ask about what's happening? I don't know.

If they did change your job, does that mean a different salary? Is it more or less than before? I don't know.

Besides The President saying he *was hired* before her inauguration; Rex was never notified of any job change. More and more people treated him as though he was an advisor to The President, but all he wanted to do was keep his head down and not have another outburst.

When The President spoke to him, he was obligated to speak back, but he wasn't sure what to do anymore.

When Rex turned onto his street, his house and front lawn were crowded with reporters and TV cameras.

8.0 YEARS AFTER OPPOSITE DAY DECLARED

Jeffery Tripp Perez

(8.0 YEARS AFTER OPPOSITE DAY DECLARED)

Jeffery Tripp Perez finally had a moment to himself after winning the nomination to be the Conservative Party candidate for President. He remembered the journey that had brought him to this point. The pivotal moment for Jeffery was his time in Branson, Missouri. Studying the teachings of Jacobs under the guidance of Major Wesley had armed Jeffery with new tools for how to live his life more in harmony with the true Conservative doctrine. That was when he became a true believer.

Jeffery brought his learnings home with him. Florida became the national model for how to push back on Liberals trampling on citizens' personal freedoms.

The ills of the Liberal world would not plague Florida. The Woke Mafia had entrenched themselves in the day-to-day operations of large cities across the country. To quote Jacobs, this meant that "crime was no longer punished. It was now rewarded." Shoplifters ran rampant with no cash bail, rapists and murderers were given sweetheart prison sentences, and the homeless walked the streets freely as though they were citizens. To use an analogy from Jacobs, "the Woke Mafia slithered their serpentine bodies across the necks of large cities for decades and were now starting to squeeze."

Jeffery took measures to stop this insanity before it took hold in Florida. His first action was to double the punishment for shoplifting.

But when that wasn't enough to deter all shoplifters, Jeffery decided to take away shoplifters' means of harming the public. Jeffery had the Florida Legislature pass a law that made shoplifting punishable by behanding. However, as per usual, the Supreme Court was called in to determine if Jeffery had the ability to protect the personal freedoms of law-abiding citizens.

But Jeffery's approach to law and order was not the only way Jacobs' teaching shone through in how Jeffery governed. Jeffery was clearly on the forefront of governors who took a stand on how "the right" to abortion infringed on citizens' personal freedoms. But thanks to Jacobs' teachings, Jeffery was able to take it one step further.

According to Jacobs, the root cause of abortion could all be traced back to the temptation of man by woman. It was woman who had tempted Adam with an apple, it was woman who tempted Jacobs and caused him problems with human resources at the Conservative News Network. The only way to fight abortion was to stop it at its root. Therefore, if women were prevented from tempting man, then there would be no need for abortion. That is how Jacobs came up with the Florida Modesty Laws.

Under the Florida Modesty Laws, women would be prevented from appearing in public, dressed in a manner that would tempt men. It wasn't like Jeffery didn't like the ladies. On the contrary, he loved the ladies. Billie and Wilma D. were women, and they agreed with the law, so the law must have been sensible to women as well.

However, as per usual, it was impossible to do anything in the best interests of the people without the Supreme Court sticking their nose into Florida's business. That would all change when Jeffery was The President. Then the Supreme Court would answer to him. That's how it worked. He would be their boss.

The President (She/Her) and the Davids (1/1)

(8.0 YEARS AFTER OPPOSITE DAY DECLARED)

The Davids sat with The President in an emergency meeting as she fought for her political life. Her popularity had ebbed and flowed through her first term. She had begun her Presidency with the lowest approval rating of any President in modern history, but her support grew when she changed the way she spoke and stopped posting online. While The President's popularity peaked with her enactment of the executive order to safeguard the elderly from fraud, it was short-lived and sank to a new low in the wake of the Rex Kellermam scandal.

Now Rex Kellermam's trial for treason was starting at the worst possible time for The President. With only a year until the election, the headlines from the Rex Kellermam trial would serve as a constant reminder to voters of the ugly mess.

However, the Rex Kellermam scandal was not bad for all. With Rex's absence, The President was left with little choice but to summon the Davids back to his prior advisory role. The Davids returned to his role ready to sink his teeth into the upcoming election. But the fallout from the Rex Kellermam scandal was a lot to overcome.

Another positive for the Davids was that they no longer had to huddle in dark corners to avoid sunlight during meetings. The President was aware that the Davids were sunlight impaired and ordered all windows of government buildings to be fully sealed, blocking out all UV rays, to make a more inclusive environment.

The Davids paced feverishly around the room, basking in the freedom of movement The President's inclusivity had afforded him. David G. was gravely concerned about The President's prospects. "Madam President, you must say or do something. It doesn't matter what, but anything to drown out the headlines from the Rex Kellermam trial."

The President recoiled at hearing Rex's name aloud. Her loyal Rex Kellermam, or should she say Rex Keller if that was even his real name. She felt like such a fool. He was the worst kind of friend; he was an unfriend. But had he just been an unfriend, that would have been less harmful. He was a two-faced fake friend. The President didn't like Rex at all. In fact, she would go so far as to say she unliked him. She normally tried to respond to haters with magnanimity, but she could not overcome the hate in this case.

Her despair at Rex's deception turned to anger and then determination. She looked forward to seeing Rex face the consequences for his actions, but there was something more important than that. She couldn't allow this to be the end of her. She knew that the unlikely circumstances that had brought her to this point could all disappear just as easily as they had come, but not like this. She couldn't give Rex that satisfaction. She would do anything to avoid it.

"Mention not that two-faced Cassius again. While I will do my best in this matter to remain disinterested, I cannot help but admit my wish that the court's justice be most sanguinary and cruel. That vile intriguer will not prove my ruin."

David W. saw an opening to seize on the passions of The President. "Madam President, Jeffery Tripp Perez is making great headway with his laws. You must say or do something about them. Normally we would suggest just saying the opposite of whatever he says, but with the trial of you-know-who starting, you may need to go further than that."

The President sighed. The new laws that were being passed in Florida were so hurtful to so many, it made The President want to unfollow the whole state. But what about rising above the haters and responding to their hate with magnanimity? That strategy had worked for her in the Tennessee Valley, so why not try it here? Wouldn't responding with opposites just be stooping to Jeffery Tripp Perez's level? Wouldn't it be better not to dignify them with a response?

"Is it not below our station to respond in kind? It appears the only outcome of this experiment in opposites has been the widening of political vicissitudes amongst parties, the ends of which satiate only the most extreme of partisans. Have we not slipped into a wretched sort of despotism where the voices of the most ardent factionalists reign over the will of the majority?"

David G. took a deep breath. He paused for a moment to give weight to The President's concerns and then said, "No, I don't think so."

The President looked pensively at the Davids. "OK, how should we respond?"

Shawn Bennet

(8.0 YEARS AFTER OPPOSITE DAY DECLARED)

hawn Bennet smacked the top of a table that stood on the side of the entrance to his office. He knew it was immature, but it was the third time this week that he hit his knee on the table while he blindly fumbled for the light switch in his office. It was the middle of the day, but it was pitch black in Shawn's office, due to The President's executive order to shut all natural light out of government buildings.

Shawn knew that hitting his knee was only part of the reason why he smacked the table. He was pissed off from the meeting he just had with the Davids. Shawn couldn't believe what he was being asked to support. The President wanted to push through laws that would go further than just offsetting the harsh laws in Florida.

The President wanted Congress to pass legislation that would make it impossible for states to enforce any laws on shoplifting, nationally legalize all current narcotics, and reduce all felonies other than rape and murder to misdemeanors. On top of that, The President wanted to make a national standard for abortions of up to two years after a child's birth.

Shawn didn't want to take part in this. This was part of the disturbing and intensifying nature of Opposite Day. Every law that was put in place by one side was knocked down by the other side in a matter of months or years. But knocking down the law wasn't enough. The other side wouldn't stop until they ensured that the reverse of the rule that they had just knocked down was put in place. As a result, Liberal areas were becoming lawless hellscapes, while Conservative areas were becoming increasingly unwelcoming and intolerant.

The only exception to this rule was the executive order protecting senior citizens from fraud. Shawn couldn't figure out why, but for some reason, that was the only law that Liberals had put in place that Conservatives did not attack. Shawn thought maybe Conservatives weren't focused on it, and he was possibly in the clear.

On top of everything, Shawn received a call on his way back from his meeting with the Davids. It was from Rex Kellermam's, or Rex Keller's, or whatever his name was lawyer, asking for a meeting. Shawn had no idea why they were contacting him, but he didn't want any part in this nonsense. He agreed to the meeting, hoping he could settle any issues and wouldn't be dragged into court.

The Committee to Unify National Tories

(8.0 YEARS AFTER OPPOSITE DAY DECLARED)

Billie and Wilma D. finished putting on their modesty outfits. They were shrouded from head to toe with only their eyes and mouths uncovered. Originally, modesty outfits were only supposed to have eye holes, but Jeffery was concerned that covering one's mouth could be considered a form of mask, and masks were still illegal in Florida. After Jeffery consulted with Jacobs, they decided that it would be more in line with the true Conservative teachings to leave the mouth uncovered.

Billie and Wilma D. didn't know what the big deal about the modesty outfits was. Liberals complained that it trampled on womens' freedoms. But it wasn't like all women were forced to wear modesty outfits. Modesty outfits were only necessary for women in the top quartile of attractiveness, and this was decided by Jacobs on a case-by-case basis. Jacobs couldn't have been clearer on this point. He now spent a majority of his time personally judging each case on whether or not a modesty outfit was needed, and to Jacobs' credit, he was thorough in coming to his final judgement.

The only thing women were asked to do is send Jacobs a picture of themselves in various states of undress with a list of their measurements, likes, and dislikes. It wasn't a big deal; Jacobs could have been a doctor if he wanted to.

Billie and Wilma D. felt that if anything, the modesty outfits gave them more freedom. By covering up their appearance, they no longer had to worry about their status as an imperfection in the algorithm. Finally, they did not have to hide their superior intelligence. Now that they were free to show their intelligence, they could reconcile some of the inconsistencies in Conservative teachings that had gnawed at them for so long.

At the top of their list was the executive order to protect senior citizens from fraud. This was a classic example of Liberal over-regulation and a government handout to a special interest group. According to Conservative teachings, over-regulation and handouts were bad. Based on the parameters of the algorithm, Billie and Wilma D. would have to fight this executive order, take it down, and then put in a law that more than offset the executive order's benefits to the elderly.

They would parlay this into the largest Conservative legislative coup of all time. The law they would put in place to offset the executive order would attack the largest government handout of them all. Billie and Wilma D. could not understand how Conservatives did not fight against Social Security and Medicare benefits. Did they not contradict true Conservative teachings? Why had they never fought this before? Shouldn't their Conservative base be screaming for an end to these programs?

Rex Keller

Rex Keller stood at the doorway of his cell, surveying the room for threats. There were threats all around. To his left were rapists and thieves. To his right were murderers and con artists. That is not what concerned Rex.

Rex faced a charge of high treason, which, if he were convicted, could mean the death penalty. That is not what concerned Rex either.

Rex felt a sense of doom that he couldn't shake. It wasn't the criminals that he was surrounded by, or the accusation of treason that he faced. It was much worse than that.

At first, when Rex was charged with treason, he was hopeful that this was all a case of mistaken identity, and he'd be back home soon enough. After his first meeting with his lawyer, Rex became convinced that it no longer mattered. Nothing mattered. They were all doomed.

Jeffery Tripp Perez and
The Committee to Unify National Tories

(8.0 Years after Opposite Day Declared)

"I am so sorry; Mr. Jacobs cannot come to the phone. He left strict instructions that he will be doing modesty outfit examinations for the rest of the week and is not to be disturbed." Jacobs' assistant felt incredibly uncomfortable not putting the call through, but Jacobs had been clear on his instructions. Jacobs took his role as assessor for modesty outfits very seriously. He locked himself in his bathroom to ensure he had privacy and pored over pictures for his modesty examinations exhaustively, to make sure he got it right. He sometimes wouldn't come out for days. There was no way she could interrupt him, not even for Jeffery Tripp Perez.

Jeffery looked over at Billie and Wilma D., "It doesn't look like he can come to the phone."

Jeffery was desperate to consult with Jacobs. Billie and Wilma D. had come to him with a proposal to attack the executive order protecting senior citizens from fraud, and then go after Social Security and Medicare. Jeffery couldn't help but see the logic in their point, but something about the idea seemed off. He wanted to consult with Jacobs before he gave the green light, but Jacobs had been so tied up in his modesty outfit examinations recently that he barely came out of the bathroom to eat or sleep.

Jeffery admired Jacob's dedication, but he, Billie D., and Wilma D. had been trying to reach him for weeks. Jeffery didn't know why he was waffling so much on this decision. He was a man of action. Waffling had never been his problem, but he was missing that last bit of courage he needed to pull the trigger.

Billie and Wilma D. wondered the same. If anything, Jeffery had been a loose cannon in the past. They thought it would be a layup getting him to act on their proposal. But no matter how clear their logic was, they couldn't get Jeffery to make the final move. Billie and Wilma D. realized they were missing something from their normal ability to motivate Jeffery to act.

They had noticed this issue for the last few months, ever since they first wore the modesty outfits. Jeffery looked like he was about to give the go-ahead when he began to tremble. Billie and Wilma D. had never seen Jeffery show fear so openly before. When they saw Jeffery shaking in fear, they realized the issue with his decision-making process.

While the modesty outfits had given Billie and Wilma D. the ability to flex their intellectual muscle more firmly over Jeffery, the outfits had reduced their ability to control Jeffery's actions. Jeffery no longer felt as strong a need to impress them. In order to get Jeffery to act, he needed the bravery that came from not wanting to act like a chicken-shit in front of attractive women.

Billie and Wilma D. stepped forward towards Jeffery. They then unfurled the head coverings of their modesty garments so that Jeffery could see their faces. They knew this was an apostasy according to Conservative teachings, but they saw no other way.

Billie D. said, "Our logic is sound. You should proceed."

Wilma D. then jumped in to assure Jeffery. "I concur."

When Jeffery saw Billie and Wilma D.'s faces, he was aghast. He knew they were heretics, but at the same time, he found himself with a feeling he had had in the past. Jeffery immediately stopped shaking, stood tall, and said, "Yea, what are we waiting for? Let's do this."

Wesley Johnston, Jeffery Tripp Perez, and The Committee to Unify National Tories

(8.0 Years after Opposite Day Declared)

The Nurse let Jeffery Tripp Perez, Billie D., and Wilma D. into Major Johnston's room. Major Johnston had ordered the three of them down to Branson, Missouri as soon as he watched Jeffery's press conference attacking Social Security and Medicare.

All three of them knew this was serious but didn't know what the urgency was about. Jeffery marched into Major Johnston's room, stood at attention, and opened his mouth. He stood there with his mouth open for about a minute before he realized that Major Johnston had not spit directly into his mouth. In fact, Jeffery had not even heard Major Johnston collect the mucus in his throat to spit into his mouth.

Jeffery looked down at Major Johnston. Major Johnston was staring daggers at him.

Major Johnston then picked up the large remote which was lying on his armrest and muted the television. He had wrapped up his previous meeting, but it was not with Jacobs. Jacobs had dedicated all his time recently to his modesty inspections for women and therefore had not been on air in weeks. After Major Johnston pressed mute, he stood up slowly. Upon seeing him try to stand, his nurse rushed over to help, but Major Johnston waved her off.

Major Johnston slowly lifted himself out of his chair. Jeffery, Billie D., and Wilma D. had never seen him stand before. When Major

Johnston was fully out of his seat, he grabbed a walker that was next to his reclining chair and made his way over to where Jeffery stood.

Major Johnston walked as close to Jeffery as he could, looked up and said, "You think you're one slick motherfucker, don't you?"

Jeffery was flummoxed. "Sir, no sir, Major Wesley," Jeffery enthusiastically shouted back.

Major Johnston shot Jeffery a look, "Don't you call me Major Wesley. When I speak, you address me as Sir or Major Johnston."

"Sir, yes sir, Major Johnston," Jeffery replied, feeling hurt by the loss of informality.

"So if you don't think you're one slick motherfucker, then you must think I am a dumb son of a bitch. Is that what you think, Perez?"

Jeffery kept a stoic look on his face. "Sir, no sir, Major Johnston." Jeffery had never seen the Major this angry at anyone of the Conservative persuasion before, but he still didn't have the slightest idea why Major Johnston was angry.

"So if you don't think you're one slick motherfucker, and you don't think I am a dumb son of a bitch, then you must be the stupidest pretty boy pansy ass I have ever laid my eyes on." Major Johnston was now shaking with anger as he followed up, "Are you the stupidest pretty boy pansy ass I have ever laid my eyes on?"

Jeffery tried to remain stoic, but he was clearly choking back sadness. "Sir, if you say so sir," he shouted back. Jeffery looked over to Billie and Wilma D. hoping to regain the courage to keep the sadness from showing on his face, but they were both wearing their modesty outfits and Jeffery didn't have the same motivation to look tough in front of them. Modesty outfit mandates in Florida were still pending with the Supreme Court. However, they were gaining voluntary popularity in several Conservative enclaves throughout the country. Still Billie and Wilma D. felt they should wear their modesty outfits to the meeting out of strict adherence to Conservative teachings.

"Don't you look over at them, I haven't said, at ease," Major Johnston shouted at Jeffery. Without a word, Jeffery shot his eyes away from Billie and Wilma D. and back to Major Johnston. "You eyeballing me now son? You better not be," Major Johnston threatened.

"Sir, excuse me, if I may jump in," Billie D. said as she stepped forward.

"Well if it isn't Mrs. Roboto herself. How did you let this happen? You were supposed to have an eye on your rising star. I told you from the get-go that he wasn't a true Conservative."

"Sir, we are unsure of what you are talking about," Wilma D. now said as she stepped forward.

Major Johnston's head started shaking with anger, and a vein that was previously not visible before appeared on his forehead. "You mean to tell me you just alienated the entire base of the Conservative Party, and you don't understand what you did?"

"Sir, sorry I'm having trouble understanding you. Would you please rephrase or try again later?" Wilma D. asked.

Major Johnston now looked more exasperated than angry. "When you attacked fraud protections for senior citizens, Social Security, and Medicare, that tends to alienate senior citizens, the lifeblood of the Conservative Party."

"Oh, OK, got it," Wilma D. replied.

At that moment, the Conservative Conservative News Network came back from commercial. Major Johnston looked at the TV. "Now look, you buffoons have made me late for my next meeting. Stick around. I'm not done with any of you."

Major Johnston sat back down in his reclining chair, paying careful attention to his next meeting.

Jeffery, Billie D., and Wilma D. all stood silent as the Conservative Conservative News Network played. The coverage of Jeffery's attack on fraud protection for senior citizens, Social Security, and Medicare on the Conservative Conservative News Network seemed all over the place. The hosts were rudderless, as if they didn't know how to react. Some reporters applauded the move while others castigated it. Jeffery found the whole affair of hosts taking different opinions regarding his announcement to be quite unseemly. Jeffery felt that the Conservative Conservative hosts disagreeing with each other lacked a certain gentility that he looked for when addressing members of the same party. He thought to himself that he would have much preferred if the hosts all liked or even all hated what he said.

The whole time Major Johnston watched the Conservative Conservative News Network, he cursed at the TV. But unlike before, when Jeffery and Major Johnston had watched the network together, this time Major Johnston's curses were not always aimed at the targets of the program. This time, some of his curses were aimed at the program itself.

When the program went back to commercial, Major Johnston looked angrier than before. Billie D., picking up on context clues, sensed that Major Johnston was frustrated with them and decided to assuage his concerns before he could lash out. "Major Johnston, during your last meeting, we crunched the numbers again, and still do not understand your frustration. Our math was simple. Conservatives hate large government spending and handouts. Deficit spending on Social Security and Medicare are some of the largest sources of government spending, iteration error, old people are Conservatives, old people depend on Social Security and Medicare."

Jeffery didn't fully understand that math, but he was relieved that Billie and Wilma D. were still on his side. He felt his confidence come back. "So you see, Major Johnston, it's just the math. You can't argue with it," Jeffery said, regaining his previous swagger.

Major Johnston shot to his feet with incredible agility and bypassed the use of his walker. He got right in Jeffery, Billie D., and Wilma D.'s faces, the vein on his forehead was more present, and his right eye was nearly bulging out of his socket. "You fucking maggots

... " But before he could finish his sentence, the TV blared the theme song for the Conservative Conservative News Network. Commercials had only started a few seconds ago, but they were coming back early, which indicated some form of special report or breaking news.

When the music stopped, Jacobs appeared on the screen. He was unshaven and glassy eyed. His blazer was askew, and his shirt looked creased and untucked in places as if he had rushed to put it on. Jeffery realized that Jacobs' assistant must have finally interrupted him in the bathroom while he was conducting women's modesty outfit examinations. Jeffery really admired Jacobs' dedication.

Jacobs looked solemn as he faced the cameras. He cleared his throat as he prepared to speak.

"It is with great sadness that I report tonight that there is a heretic among us." Jacob's voice cracked as if he had not spoken in some time. He cleared his throat again, "A one-time friend has turned his back on true Conservative Conservative teachings and has chosen the ways of the Philistines. However, fear not my friends, because as we cast one out, we bring another in. The Conservative Conservative movement is bigger than just one man. However, I would be remiss not to mention that it would be unfair to blame Jeffery Tripp Perez solely for his transgressions. Jeffery, as is so often the case, was led astray by not one, but two women. While our modesty outfits are in place to prevent this, our current design has a major flaw. It still allows for temptation, not from female looks or feminine wiles, but from female mouths. That is why tonight, I have two announcements. The first is that I will be restarting the examination process of all women for modesty outfits, and those modesty outfits will now include mouth coverings. The second announcement is that I am supporting a new Conservative Conservative candidate for President to stand against the left-leaning Jeffery Tripp Perez and The President. That candidate is a man of integrity, a man of passion, a man of good Conservative Conservative common decency. He is none other than last year's 'Politician of the Year' award winner, your friend and mine, Ted Cruise."

Ted Cruise then appeared by video conference. He was sporting a full-on smirk as he began his remarks. "Ford Ranger, Ford F-150, Ford Super Duty, Ford EcoSport, Ford Escape, Ford Edge, Ford Bronco…"

Major Johnston eased back into his chair during Jacobs' comments. He sat back and watched Ted Cruise's remarks with a proud grin on his face. As Ted Cruise spoke, Major Johnston said out loud, but to no one in particular, and especially not to Jeffery, Billie D., and Wilma D., "See, he's only doing American cars tonight. This guy Ted Cruise, he gets it."

20.0 YEARS BEFORE OPPOSITE DAY DECLARED

Shawn Bennet and Charles Roan
(20.0 YEARS BEFORE OPPOSITE DAY DECLARED)

The smell hit Shawn more like a quick jab than a full punch when he walked into the room. Shawn hadn't smelled anything like it in five years. It wasn't pungent enough to be a stench, although some might call it that. The smell didn't demand the full attention of all your senses the entire time you were in the room, it was more subtle. It lingered, reminding you of its presence every time you had the audacity to let your guard down and pay attention to something else. It was more of an odor, and unlike a stench, its presence did not demand its immediate eradication. It could be tolerated, and therefore it remained, a constant reminder to anyone in the room of why they were there.

Shawn correctly placed the last time he encountered the odor to the last days he spent with his Grandpa James. Now Shawn was taking part in the same ritual for his Grandpa Charles, who was now in his last days. Shawn was struck by the similarities of the rituals for two men who had lived such different lives. Besides the smell, both men experienced moments of lucidity which were fleeting, followed by the awkward waiting. Everyone realized they wouldn't get better, but Shawn wondered if his grandfathers realized it as well. What was the outcome they were hoping for? Was it just a peaceful death? If they didn't realize, did they find it odd that family members who had visited on a monthly, quarterly, or annual basis were now coming almost every day?

But Grandpa James and Grandpa Charles had other similarities. Both lived to be 97 years old. Even though one was rich and the other was poor, they were both minorities that lived in Tulsa and were subjected to unspeakable violence in the early parts of their lives. However, that is where their similarities ended.

Grandpa James was financially ruined when his family's pharmacy was burned down in the Tulsa Race Massacre, but his family members' lives had been spared in the violence. Grandpa James attributed the violence to the white citizens of Tulsa not wanting the residents of the Greenwood district as neighbors. However, rather than shutting people out, Grandpa James came away focusing his life on friends and neighbors, making sure to unquestioningly welcome everyone in. When Shawn was younger, he admired this about Grandpa James. But, as Shawn got older, he saw Grandpa James' trusting nature turn from an asset to a liability. Shawn knew that Grandpa James lived the end of his life in squalor because he had taken his trusting nature too far.

Grandpa Charles on the other hand lost his entire family but came away as the sole inheritor of his family's oil property. However, his guardian's betrayal taught Grandpa Charles never to trust anyone. As a result, Grandpa Charles spent his life keeping friends and neighbors away. While he did not live the end of his life in squalor like Grandpa James, he did live it alone.

Shawn marveled at the different paths these two men had taken. How each of them reacted logically to what happened to them, but how they both took it too far and suffered as a result.

8.0 YEARS AFTER OPPOSITE DAY DECLARED

Shawn Bennet and Rex Keller

(8.0 YEARS AFTER OPPOSITE DAY DECLARED)

Shawn Bennet walked into the prison meeting room to find Rex Keller and his lawyer, Max Triboro, sitting on the same side of a table, waiting for him.

Shawn felt uneasy going into the meeting. First of all, it was in a prison, and secondly it was with Rex Keller, one of the most infamous people in the country. Shawn didn't have the best political instincts, but he knew he was screwed if it got out that he was meeting with Rex. Still, he went hoping he could avoid getting himself dragged into this mess in court. "Hey, look, I'm not really sure why you asked to meet, but no offense, I would really love not to be involved."

While Shawn maintained skepticism of law enforcement, he figured that anyone charged with treason was most likely guilty.

Rex looked at his hands, which were shackled to the table in front of him, and then looked up at Shawn, "Thanks for coming. But this isn't about the case." Shawn could see that jail life had hardened Rex. Rex was more assertive when he spoke and did not survey the room as much.

Max shook his head in disbelief. "Rex, you don't have to do this. There is no reason for you not to fight." Then Max looked over towards Shawn. "Congressman Bennet. This was all a case of mistaken identity. Rex didn't pretend to be an advisor to The President. She just kept talking to him. He thought he was still a member of the Secret Service."

Shawn gave Max a very skeptical look. Then he thought back to his meetings with The President and Rex. Shawn remembered how Rex was situated far off in every meeting and looked uncomfortable when The President spoke to him. Shawn just thought Rex was a weird guy, but come to think of it, that story did resonate.

But Rex cut Max off. "We didn't ask you to come down here because of the trial. Whatever happens to me is unimportant. We are all doomed. That's what matters."

Shawn was at first relieved to hear that Rex was not looking to drag him into this mess, but as soon as the initial relief passed, Shawn worried about what it was they were after. "Then I'm confused. What could you possibly want with me?"

Max sensed Shawn's weariness. He thought the message might sound less crazy coming from him than from Rex. "Congressman Bennet, you are the man that stood up to HUAC. The country needs your help again."

Shawn was concerned about the legal advice Rex was receiving. "Excuse me. I'm no expert on this, but Rex, don't both of you have more pressing issues? If I'm correct, you face the death penalty. Shouldn't your lawyer be focused on that?"

Rex knew he had promised Max he would leave most of the talking to him, but Rex couldn't hold back his concern. "If you don't act, we are all dead anyways!" he shouted.

Shawn thought the pressure of the situation was getting to Rex. Rex must have been having some sort of psychotic episode. Any inkling of doubt that Shawn had as to Rex's guilt faded with Rex's outburst.

But then Rex said, "I've seen it in your face in meetings. You are confused, right? You feel that you are the only one who doesn't get it. What is happening, why people are acting the way they are? When was the last time anything made sense to you? You aren't the only one."

Shawn paused. Shawn was in a constant state of confusion, and Rex was the first person to also admit that he didn't understand any of this nonsense. Even though Shawn was still dubious about Rex and Max, Rex's comment sparked a kindred feeling. Shawn felt that since Opposite Day started, people were only focused on being opposed to something that was wrong, rather than doing what they thought was right. This was the first time he did not feel alone in that sentiment.

"So, what would you like me to do? Let me guess. Turn Conservative or even Conservative Conservative?" Shawn said, keeping up his façade of skepticism.

Rex shook his head, "No! You're not getting it." Rex then calmed himself, realizing his emotions were alienating Shawn. "That would be more of the same. Just doing the opposite of something you think is wrong. If you do that, we are doomed either way. Liberals kill you by caring too much, Conservatives kill you by not caring at all. Even though both approaches are opposite, they lead to the same result."

Shawn laughed in agreement, but then again realized he was commiserating with one of the most reviled men in the country.

Max decided to take over the reins of the conversation from Rex. "Congressman Bennet. Do you know why I sought Rex out as a client? I, like Rex, was a victim of Alice Hershe. I have found countless others like myself and Rex. From the widow of a mattress retailer to the residents of the Tennessee Valley. Looking at the news recently, Conservatives aren't much better. Families of the victims of the Spit Brothers pandemic, refugees from Florida's modesty laws, and even the elderly in your own district who fell prey to the great Tulsa telemarketing and pyramid scheme boon."

Shawn listened to the list of victims, feeling responsible for the elderly in his district who were harmed by telemarketers and pyramid schemes. If only he had been more savvy about Opposite Day back then, he never would have said anything, and they would have been fine. "Look, I don't even get what's going on. How can I help when I am the only one that's confused?"

Rex interrupted again, "Your confusion is what sets you apart. That's what can save us. You understand what is going on better than anyone because you are confused."

Shawn shook his head in frustration. "I'm the only one confused, so I'm the only one who understands? C'mon … Did you really bring me down here just to pull this Opposite Day crap?"

Rex tried to keep himself from getting excited and in the most earnest tone he could muster, said, "This isn't about opposites. When something is confusing, you should be confused. Logical people can have different answers to the same problem. That doesn't make them opposites. The fact that they are now classified as opposites is confusing to you."

Max shrugged. "In all my searching, you are the only person I have found in a position of power who is confused. You could say something, run for something. Just do something to challenge these maniacs."

Shawn couldn't believe it. He was considering political advice from someone on trial for treason. "But if I say or do something as you suggest, what good would that be? You two are the only others I have found who feel this way."

Rex and Max looked at each other and then back at Shawn. Then Max said, "That is the dumbest thing I have heard in years. Everyone feels this way."